think

UNthink

rediscover your
creative genius

erikwahl

CROWN
BUSINESS
NEW YORK

Published in the United States by Crown Business, an imprint of the
Crown Publishing Group, a division of Random House, Inc., New York.
www.crownpublishing.com

CROWN BUSINESS is a trademark and CROWN and the Rising Sun
colophon are registered trademarks of Random House, Inc.

Crown Business books are available at special discounts for bulk
purchases for sales promotions or corporate use. Special editions,
including personalized covers, excerpts of existing books, or books with
corporate logos, can be created in large quantities for special needs. For
more information, contact Premium Sales at (212) 572-2232 or e-mail
specialmarkets@randomhouse.com.

Library of Congress Cataloging-in-Publication Data
Wahl, Erik.
    Unthink / Erik Wahl.—First edition.
    pages cm
    1. Creative thinking. 2. Creative ability in business.
    3. Organizational change. I. Title.
    HD53.W34 2013
    153.3'5—dc23   2013004800

ISBN 978-0-7704-3400-7
eISBN 978-0-7704-3402-1

Printed in the United States of America

Book design by Lauren Dong
Illustrations by Erik Wahl
Jacket design by Via Design

10 9 8 7 6 5 4 3 2 1

First Edition

They say that dedicating a book is one of the most exquisite acts of love one can perform. Without hesitation I dedicate this book to my artistic inspiration, my best friend, my unconditional lover, my wife of eighteen years, Tasha. Come hell or high water I will forever dance through the minefields and long to be tangled up in your arms.

contents

introduction
A Bigger Canvas:
My Story

The world is but a canvas to our imaginations.
—Henry David Thoreau

We secretly believe that creative genius is reserved for the chosen few—for the poets, the painters, the writers. The truth is that breakthrough creativity is in all of us. It *is* us. It is the process through which you and I discover all we were meant to be and do. Without it you and I are little more than waves tossed about by the Great Sea, arriving where the winds and currents of our life funnel us. Breakthrough creativity is the force that changes that tide. It is the daring ship that rises up on the Great Sea and employs the wind and waves to its advantage as it sails in search of new and better lands. This is as vital to your happiness as it is to the value of your work.

Don't be fooled. Creativity does not reside in one special person. And it is not in one special place. It is everywhere and in everyone who has the courage to tap into his or her full potential. Creative genius is born of the desire for adventure that never leaves you . . . the ever-present wanderlust that beckons you from your tidy, predictable days . . . the insatiable curiosity that forever hopes—forever longs—for life to be bigger and more vibrant and more meaningful than the one you currently live. Following those promptings is your path to freedom. It begins when you see yourself for who you truly are.

You are a fearless artist capable of original, breakthrough ideas and solutions at any moment, on any day. But over time, you have been steered away from venturing, wandering, and wondering. You've been taught to think logically, but not daringly, concretely, or instinctively. You've all but forgotten the artistic tools with which you were born.

Once you remember—once you learn to unthink how you live and work—everything will change.

What you should know from the start is that I have not always been an artist. I was not born with artistic skills and I wasn't very good at art as a child. At least that's what was told to me by a well-meaning elementary school teacher wanting to direct me toward more practical pursuits. It wasn't until years later, when I finally lost my safe identity, that I redis-covered my fearless creativity—that whole and confident identity, hidden inside us all, that compels us into the unique quest for which we were each made.

Let me tell you my whole story. This could be your story too.

I was good at school. Efficient at testing, I measured my self-worth and value as a student, and as a man, the way I was taught to: by the grades I received. I was a rule follower—operationally efficient. A teacher's dream.

In perfecting this persona I became a purveyor of no-nonsense order and execution. There was little value in creativity—it didn't offer a structure that allowed for a clear-cut way to measure my progress. And so I consented to becoming successful by being the most efficient rule follower around.

After securing my college degree I found a comfortable job that played well to my tidy work ethic. I earned a decent salary and a job title that made me feel respectable at social gatherings. I religiously followed the standard corporate system and was rewarded with standard corporate success. But the cost of the journey was the loss of the part of me that kept life beautiful and fascinating and fun. Looking back, I realize my career stability was becoming a dangerous addiction that was keeping me from taking any real risk or pursuing any real adventure.

I was achieving what the world called progress, but was I really going anywhere I wanted to be?

Though I wouldn't admit it then, after a decade in the business world I still couldn't kick a certain feeling that my best talents were wasting away inside me. I was successful but my day-to-day life was less and less satisfying.

In an effort to overcome this lackluster existence, I began to feed my ego. I bolstered my public image and tried to find the satisfaction I was lacking by overextending myself financially in what I thought were prudent, leveraged investments to puff up my brand. In truth, I wasn't trying to prove myself to the world. I was trying to prove myself to me.

Then it happened. The dot.com bubble that had been so cooperative in helping me build my fortress of security finally burst. The financial world collapsed, my career went into a tailspin, and I lost everything: my money, my investments, my security, and, ultimately, my identity.

It was a gut-wrenching and nauseating experience. I was forced to start from ground zero at thirty years old, with a wife and three children under five years old. At night I was especially tormented, lying awake obsessing about my losses.

For someone like me, who had spent a lifetime fighting weakness, my vulnerability was a new, unfamiliar, awkward feeling. Ironically, it was this weakness, this reluctant confession of need, that would serve as my escape hatch to a new life.

I finally admitted that my days hadn't been inspiring . . . they'd just been okay . . . serviceable mostly . . . they paid the bills and gave me a sense that I was making progress. But that progress didn't move me.

That is when I woke from my standardized slumber and began to explore. I became a child again.

My frustration and anger led me to self-reflection, then inspiration. I determined to break free from the addiction to security that had lulled the passionate version of me to sleep. I rebelled against my elementary school teacher's conclusion that art "just wasn't my thing" and reawakened the artist inside me.

"All change is preceded by crisis," wrote Søren Kierkegaard. My crisis was an utter but necessary loss of the framework through which I viewed myself and my work. Suddenly I saw that the processes I had ordered into easily repeatable patterns had formed a ceiling over my potential. I realized that my dreams were being held captive by convention, and my imagination had been lulled to sleep by the potion of predictability.

I had been seduced into a life of little conviction—a logical, systematic existence. My best talents had been buried beneath well-intentioned but ultimately lifeless rules meant to hem me into the corporate fabric.

What felt like an existence I controlled actually controlled me. My pillars of success were truly walls that kept me from seeing my own horizon. I could see only what was inside those walls. It was as if I were living in a cabin in the most pristine mountain range in the world, only the cabin didn't have doors or windows. I therefore made do with what was inside the cabin, never realizing that just outside was more beauty, adventure, and meaning in every direction than I could imagine.

Now the cupboards were bare and I had no more wood to light a fire. My choice was simple: stay inside and starve to death or get outside the walls and find a way to survive.

I chose to kick down the walls of my security and explore what was on the other side. It marked a full-scale rebellion against the sheltered life I'd lived so long.

Painting became my rehab.

With no formal training, I picked up some paint supplies and poured myself onto the canvas. No rules. No standards. Being messy, spreading paint with brushes and hands, was cathartic. My discontent was being exorcised. But it was more than therapy. I found painting fascinating and beautiful. It called to me in a way nothing had in years. I started hanging out with local artists. Dialoguing with artists. Exploring ideas with artists. My mind started to expand in every direction. I once again began to drink in life like a child.

Art intoxicated me—as a craft and as a way of life. I began to understand art not only as a noun—a finished piece of work—but also as a verb—a leaping, diving, daring way of living. Whether I could make it a career remained to be seen. Still, the opportunity to remake myself into something more true seemed a risk worth taking. Less risk, in fact, than returning to who I had been. I dove headlong into rediscovering myself—in particular, that part of me that longed for exploration without time lines . . . imagination without boundaries . . . execution without rules.

But I wasn't seeing the whole picture before me. The more I explored the art community, the more I realized that it also had limitations. While many of the artists I met had incredible originality and skill, they lacked the training and tools to make a living. Their creativity did not translate into creative commerce, primarily because they assumed that businesses were built on passion and ideas alone. As a result these artists often succumbed to the cliché that they were obscure because the world simply didn't understand its need for them.

Having come from a corporate gig, I knew better, from a philosophical and practical standpoint. But what then was my stance? If I didn't fully buy into corporate conventions *or* the artistic community, was I a corporate anarchist? An artistic bureaucrat? I found myself caught between an appreciation of corporate know-how and an appreciation of artistic imagination, without a full faith in either.

That's when it hit me. My faith was not in one or the other. It was in both.

I realized that our greatest career potential isn't reached by conventional, critical thinking alone. It's also not reached by innovative, unconventional thinking alone. Our greatest personal potential is reached when unbridled imagination is applied with critical competence and when business acumen is embodied with artistic finesse.

The challenge we face in the corporate world is that we have long been programmed to carry out our jobs with only one mind-set: the conventional, critical one. And it's killing our ability to create unique ideas and ultimately destroying our potential.

The short story goes like this: Our education taught us to memorize the predetermined answer or study the predetermined method in order to deliver the predetermined solution. There was nearly always one right way to one right answer, and an A+ job meant finding and then following that path repeatedly. There was rarely if ever room for what we so fondly call "thinking outside the box." You and I were rewarded for—often literally—making a check mark *inside* the right box. We were taught to be art critics but not artists. To think but not to unthink.

When we graduated from college we received further reinforcement of this philosophy of progress. We were given a concrete job description and with it a predetermined list of expectations that included following a protocol and meeting a quota. We were then trained by someone who had memorialized our job's methodology for success. Our responsibility was simple: replicate the methodology. For this we were rewarded. Bonuses. Raises. Awards. And ultimately, promotion to a position in which more of the same was asked of us but with a higher degree of accountability.

And so you and I learned that to stabilize and grow our careers, we must comprehend and conform to what had already been done. There was little if any need to originate.

A full-scale rebellion against this system is impractical, idealistic, and unviable. The starving artist is not just hyperbole. But an expansion of conventional thinking is desperately needed.

The realization of this struck me as an epiphany. What if the artistic sensibilities that drive constant creative breakthroughs were combined with the practical business strategies that I had learned to apply so effectively? Was it even possible? And if so, what would this sort of behavior look like?

In a flurry of ideas on napkins that exploded into note cards and scratch paper spread across the kitchen floor, I scribbled without stopping and in one night captured my questions, hunches, and early conclusions on a new way of thinking about working; the dynamic tension between business sense and artistic sensibility was an intoxicating elixir. I pored over any relevant research I could find during the days and weeks that followed. Eventually an answer came nearer when I discovered that the character traits—the governing philosophies of behavior—that shaped artistic icons like

Picasso, Hemingway, and Mozart were the same ones that shaped business titans like Buffett, Jobs, and Branson. That understanding alone was eye opening. But what did it mean?

For starters, it meant that creativity had many forms and that art wasn't relegated to the walls of museums, libraries, and concert halls. It also resided in the halls of corporate headquarters. It echoed off the office walls of savvy executives and shrewd entrepreneurs.

Still, this wasn't enough. I wanted a more tangible example—someone I could relate to, someone embodying these traits who was more accessible, more relatable, than a Warren Buffett or an Ernest Hemingway. I continued my search.

The answer was in front of me all along. There was a third group who embodied these traits perhaps more freely and consistently than the icons of past and present. The kicker was that not only could I relate to the group but I was once a part of it—and so were you.

I'm talking about children.

In our early years, you and I consistently embodied the key traits that drive constant creativity. Curiosity ruled our senses. Enthusiasm ignited our actions. We did not fear what we did not know—instead we thrived on the process of discovery. We were oblivious to onlookers and untrusting of naysayers. And best of all, our imaginations were unbound.

But before you lament that those days are long gone, you should know there's an upside.

The fact that we cannot return to childhood is to our advantage. As adults, we have far more resources at our disposal. Our minds process information more quickly. Our bodies are much stronger and much more developed, and they need less sleep. In short, we are more efficient, potent beings as adults. Yes, we have far greater responsibilities too. But we also have far greater power to not only meet those responsibilities but also to change our circumstances and the circumstances of those around us.

While creativity overflows from children like a river in spring, its capacity is limited by their immature mental and physical faculties. It is also limited by the place and time in which they grow up. Steve Jobs once pointed out that had he not had access to computers when he was young, he wouldn't have explored his imagination through computing and pro-gramming. The young Einstein's parents were gatekeepers to the expression of his creative genius. Had they accepted the common conclusion about him given by his elementary school teachers, his wild mind would have likely followed a different course. Children exude creativity. But they are still children at the mercy of immaturity and the circumstances into which their parents lead or don't lead them.

On the other hand, if we can tap back into that childlike wellspring of creativity as adults with our full faculties, we can become a positive, potent force on and off the job.

As I continued to paint, sculpt, and write with this game-changing discovery bouncing off the walls of my mind, I began to organize my napkins and note cards into a presen-tation I could share with corporate audiences. My new ca-reer path was clear. I became a different brand of corporate speaker who, instead of merely reframing the old trains of thought, began challenging companies to unthink their tra-ditional ways and venture onto a new frontier governed by both business intellect and artistic intuition, corporate sense and creative sensibility. To drive home the point, I allowed my art to become a visual metaphor by painting live from the stage during each presentation, coloring each canvas in a matter of three minutes. These sixty-minute presentations to which my epiphany had led me were far more than my own job opportunity. They were the pathway to a more vibrant, more adventurous, more potent career for anyone. And the message was not just for me. It was for all willing to rediscover their fearless creativity—their whole, confident, breakthrough identity—and then let it fly. And now, a decade later, I can report that millions have.

Over that time I have learned that inspiration can always use a follow-up. From the stage, during the course of a sixty-minute performance, I can accomplish only so much. Primarily, I can inspire people to think and act more creatively, but I want to go a step further now. I want to show you how to find and release your inner artist, not just when you need to solve a work problem or nail the big ad campaign, but every day, in the biggest and littlest of ways that will brighten the color of your days and bring you a sense of wholeness and satisfaction you may not have felt for years, even decades. Rediscovering your fearless creativity can change everything from how you perceive your job to how well you do your job to why you go to work every day. It can change your life.

To get there, we need to first get clear on where you began—the artist you once were before logic and predictability took over. You need to understand your "Then" in order to comprehend the "Now" in which you currently find yourself—in which I found myself not so long ago. Once your past and present are clear, you can confidently apply the "How" of enriching your immediate future. This will require unthinking the manner in which you've learned to think and act.

It's a path I've taken, beginning in a place that I bet is not that different from where you are now. It's a path you can take too. Fearless, boundless creativity is the destination.

I will lead the way.

The journey begins now.

—Erik Wahl
San Diego, CA
September 18, 2012

SECTION one

THEN . . .
(who you were)

what was right
about you

Every child is an artist. The problem is how to remain an artist once we grow up.

— PABLO PICASSO

Ask a roomful of five-year-olds how many are artists and every hand will shoot up. Ask a roomful of thirty-five-year-olds the same question and you might get one reluctant hand. Why is that?

The answer to that question begins by understanding who you and I were as children.

For years studies have shown that you were born with an ability to initiate new ideas and solve problems uniquely. "Children have an inbuilt drive for discovery," explains Tim Seldin, president of the International Montessori Council. "This drive for discovery continues to develop as they grow and become more adventurous in the things that they try out, from making mud pies in the garden to starting a worm farm in

the living room. Children are born with marvelous imaginations and a keen desire to explore the world."[1] In other words,
you were born an artist—an individual with a large capacity
to learn, adapt, and develop new ideas and solutions at any
moment.

As a child, your brain thrived off what neurologists call
your "right hemisphere"—the part of your brain that's in
charge of intuition and creative, social, and visual skill: the
part of your brain that embraces new and unconventional
ideas, the part that is fascinated by surprise, the part that
doesn't need everything to be neat and tidy and perfectly
defined in order to find value. As a result, your mind was
an ever-looping reel of whys and, more important, *why nots.*
Curiosity was on overdrive. Imagination was rampant. Inspiration was anywhere and everywhere. The world was your
canvas and the rules of creation were few if any.

Young boys turn sticks into swords and fight imaginary
battles on a daily basis. They turn gutter streams into mighty
rivers on which to sail their paper-made ships. Adventure,
imagination, risk—these are hardwired into young boys. The
type of toys they have or the locale in which they play doesn't
matter either. If a journey beckons, they will find what they
need or make it out of anything in reach.

Boys don't need to be taught to be creative. It pours out of
them. And they are not the only ones.

Young girls transform themselves into ballerinas with lip
gloss and any dress that fans with a twirl. Their dolls and
stuffed animals become companions on a quest to find their
prince and attend the great ball. Or they too venture off into
the great unknown—to make the next great discovery, or

to find the buried treasure, or to simply explore the outer reaches of their imaginary world.

For young boys and girls alike, exploration is their daily reality.

Do you remember when your days were governed by your imagination? You could be whoever or whatever you wanted. You could travel around the world—even beyond the world—at the drop of a thought. There were no rules that said you couldn't or shouldn't because it wasn't time productive. Pragmatism, logic, and even safety did not stand in the way. You were free to sculpt your days into works of art—tangible representations of your unique creativity—filled with joy, enthusiasm, and fulfillment.

We functioned this way as kids because our worldview was incomplete. To learn and grow, we needed to be mass collectors of information through our various senses. We were learning a language. We were figuring out how to relate to others. We were discovering the laws of physics and learning how to run and jump, and to use our muscles and limbs more efficiently. In short, we were cross-training for the many scenarios life would eventually toss at us in rapid succession. Our primary environment needed to be a rich, vibrant, and imagination-fostering one.

Many companies around the world have created offices that mirror kindergarten classrooms, hoping to spark that same rich, vibrant environment of childhood. Companies like Google have used unconventional environments to help them create cutting-edge products. The company allows its engineers to spend 20 percent of their work hours exploring anything that triggers their curiosity. The freedom allows employees to work alone and focus on something that tempts their fancy. It also allows employees who wouldn't normally intersect during the workweek to sit down together and let their ideas collide. Some of Google's greatest products grew out of this freedom—Gmail, Google Earth, Google Labs, and its flagship AdSense program.

What many don't know is that while Google hasn't admitted its inspiration for its 20 percent perk, it was probably the mining and manufacturing giant 3M, which began allowing its employees to spend 15 percent of their work time exploring the recesses of their imaginations in 1948. The company wanted to stand out in a postwar America, when rigidity defined the corporate landscape. It did so and continues to do so today. Its legendary Post-it notes were birthed by an employee named Art Fry during his 15 percent exploration time; but that is only one of more than twenty-two thousand patents that have created approximately fifty thousand different products that bring in more than $20 billion annually.[2] 3M is an innovation volcano.

Could we be oversimplifying the reasons for such companies' constant creativity when we link it to their promotion of employee imagination and exploration? While there are certainly other factors that make the Googles and 3Ms of the world so hypercreative, when asked, the employees themselves, from executive to entry level, point to this free time as the major catalyst in shaping the companies' continued success. When Marissa Mayer was Google's VP of search products and user experience (she's now CEO of Yahoo!), she estimated that approximately half of Google's new products were the result of employees' 20 percent time.[3] Kurt Beinlich, a technical director for 3M, explained that his company's 15 percent time has "shaped what and who 3M is."[4]

There is something freeing, something magical, something exuberant, about an environment where we are not hemmed in by rules and time lines and are instead opened up to imagination, possibility, and learning. This describes the landscape of early childhood.

The idea of returning to childhood for wisdom is nothing new. While the world's greatest teachers and thinkers have for centuries debated every topic and philosophy under the sun, one thing they have agreed on is the need for adults to become like children again in order to not only see our days in their fullest colors but also to pull ourselves out of ruts and push us through life's challenges.

Jesus famously scolded his disciples when they kept the children in a crowd from approaching him. "Let the little children come to me," he insisted, "and do not hinder them, for the kingdom of heaven belongs to such as these."[5] Sigmund Freud lamented, "What a distressing contrast there is between the radiant intelligence of the child and the feeble mentality of the average adult." Heraclitus wrote, "Man is most nearly himself when he achieves the seriousness of a child at play." Friedrich Nietzsche asserted, "In every real man a child is hidden that wants to play." And according to Mahatma Gandhi, "The law of love could be best understood and learned through little children."

Albert Einstein once wondered how it came to be that he was the one to develop the theory of relativity. He explained, "The reason, I think, is that a normal adult never stops to think about problems of space and time. These are things which he has thought of as a child. But my intellectual development was retarded, as a result of which I began to wonder about space and time only when I had already grown up. Naturally, I could go deeper into the problem than a child with normal capabilities."[6]

In Einstein's opinion, his genius was the result of remaining childlike into his adult life. He would later famously assert that "imagination is more important than knowledge."[7] It's a surprising assertion from the iconic genius. It is also surprising to learn that Einstein was no child prodigy. He was what we would call today a remedial student and a problem child.

"Einstein was slow in learning how to speak . . . ," explains Einstein biographer Walter Isaacson. "He also had a cheeky rebelliousness toward authority. . . . But these traits helped make him a genius. His cocky contempt for authority led him to question conventional wisdom. His slow verbal development made him curious about ordinary things . . . that most adults take for granted."[8]

Fortunately for Einstein—and the world—his parents rejected the traditionalist notions that their child was problematic. They continued to support his wild mind and unconventional habits. It paid off when he was old enough to channel his artistry with more developed skill and precision.

This childlikeness—or in some respects childishness—was also responsible for the birth of what we know today as Outward Bound, the world's largest outdoor experiential-education organization with facilities in thirty countries and six continents. Today the organization's original, unorthodox training is offered through courses for corporate team building, inner-city youth, and specific populations like alcoholics and growing families. These courses are based on founder Kurt Hahn's belief that when people are reintroduced to adventure, exploration, and risk they are able to redefine or expand their perceptions of what is possible not only in their own lives but in the lives of those around them. "There is more in us than we know," he wrote. "If we can be made to see it, we will be unwilling to settle for less."[9] The name "Outward Bound" says it all. It is a nautical term coined by Sir Lawrence Holt, a British shipping baron whose money and resources helped greatly expand the organization. It was used to describe a ship leaving the safety of its harbor and embarking on the mysterious open seas. This outward-bound inclination is something you and I followed instinctively as children.

Armed with only our imagination and the basic trappings of our bedrooms, basements, or backyards, we left the safe harbor on a daily basis. We climbed on counters, then climbed trees, then attempted to scale our houses. We leapt off the bottom stairs, then the middle stairs, then the backyard fence. Dangerous, inexplicable worlds called to us. We ran faster. Flew higher. Danced harder. Yelled louder. We exhausted ourselves in exploration and innovation. And we learned more in our first seven years than we learn in any other seven-year span in our lives.

We were truly wired to create when we were young. This doesn't mean we should stop exploring, discovering, and innovating once we are older. Today's reasons for creative breakthrough may be even stronger. We should be inspired by the fact that as adults we are far more equipped to do something truly meaningful and lasting with our discoveries. Not only can we make our lives an everyday adventure; we can enlighten the lives of others too. But to achieve our full potential, we have to do away with the notion that curiosity, imagination, and exploration are child's play.

What Einstein, Nietzsche, Gandhi, and Jesus understood is that there are unspoken maxims we embrace as children that even the most educated, experienced, advanced adults should never abandon if we want our days to still fascinate and fulfill us.

1. Mystery Adds Meaning

When Isaac Newton was asked to describe his most productive days as a scientist, he explained, "I was like a boy playing on the sea-shore, and diverting myself now and then finding a smoother pebble or a prettier shell than ordinary, whilst the great ocean of truth lay all undiscovered before me." When mystery leads, curiosity follows. Whys, Why nots, and What ifs. There are few things more constant in a child's life than curiosity.

When curiosity is a driving force, a person remains interested, present, in passionate pursuit. Kids are notorious for driving their parents crazy with their incessant questions. But these questions are the reason they learn so much so quickly. They also keep life interesting.

Consider the greatest films you've seen or books you've read. It was undoubtedly the mysterious elements of them that kept your interest piqued and senses sharp in order to satisfy your curiosity. Mystery is the reason you watch an intense five-minute sequence in a film and wonder if you took a single breath. It's the reason your limbs can unknowingly fall asleep in the midst of an engaging conversation with someone you love. It's the reason we are still fascinated by other galaxies and outer space and the possibility of life on other planets. Mystery is the reason people like business tycoon Sir Richard Branson, *Titanic* and *Avatar* director James Cameron, and Amazon CEO Jeff Bezos spend millions of dollars to explore the deepest depths of the world's oceans.

There is promise in mystery: the promise of virgin paths and uncharted waters. And, if we keep searching, there is the promise of discovery. Mystery makes everything more interesting, and more interesting means more meaningful. Creativity is born of mystery.

2. Ignorance Leads to Breakthroughs

"Einstein's vast knowledge of mathematics and science increased steadily throughout his life," explains author Scott Thorpe in his book *How to Think Like Einstein*. "But when we look at Einstein's problem-solving output something seems wrong. . . . The most profound breakthroughs came during a remarkable year during the beginning of his career. But in later years, Einstein's problem solving dropped off." Thorpe goes on to describe a fascinating and revealing trend in the life of the archetypal genius. It was during his first year out of college, while he was working at the Swiss patent office "reviewing improvements to laundry wringers" and doing physics "on the side," that he discovered $E = mc^2$. He was no less brilliant in the subsequent years and in fact knew more about science and math and had more uninterrupted time to focus on his experiments alone and with the greatest fellow minds of the day. And yet, as Thorpe points out, "he didn't solve any more scientific problems."

"We would expect Einstein's problem solving to correlate with his intelligence and knowledge," concludes Thorpe. "Instead, his problem-solving ability declined as his knowledge increased. Innovation was highest when knowledge was lowest."[10]

It is the ultimate curse of knowledge: that when we know the most, we are often least able to see new solutions to old problems or new ways to approach entrenched relationships, systems, or hierarchies. Our great knowledge is often the greatest hindrance to creativity in problem solving because the thought of setting all that knowledge aside in favor of a blank slate seems ludicrous. But the blank slate is the secret weapon of every child. At that age, you had nothing to fall back on. Nothing to precolor your assumptions. No mental files to flip through. Few past experiences from which to draw conclusions.

As a child you based your conclusions on your latest exploration or experimentation. Your knowledge was real-time and constantly evolving because your mind remained flexible and able to adapt your conclusions to your latest discovery. You constantly reserved the right to withhold judgment until further review. With this open-mindedness you remained able to see things, not as you were inclined or instructed to see them, but as things really were. Perhaps even better than they were. Ignorance—even the voluntary kind—leads to breakthroughs.

3. Later Means Never

Spend an hour around any child and you know they have an unyielding tenacity. They pursue their desires in the moment they arise and do not quit until they have what they set out to get. They want it and they want it now. Later means never. While this tenacity mixed with immediacy can drive a parent mad and lead to disciplining a child, it has a positive side. It is the reason children are masters at spontaneity. They are up for anything, anytime—especially before the requirements of school give them reasons to say no.

Ice cream at 7:00 A.M.? Absolutely.

Trampoline at 10:00 P.M.? Why not.

Song in the middle of a crowded restaurant? Which one would you like to hear?

As children get older, they become more aware of others' opinions and the expected etiquette of given situations. Before then, however, there are no self- or socially imposed limits on when and where fun, beauty, and breakthroughs can happen.

The idea of lucky breaks has been prevalent in our society for some time—especially when describing actors and performing artists. The truth, however, is that most of these so-called breaks were the result of individuals exploring possibilities spontaneously, in the moment they arose.

In his book *Earning Serendipity,* author Glenn Llopis cites some of the most well-known recipients of spontaneity's rewards. "An apple fell from a tree," writes Llopis, "and a man saw something more than bothersome fruit. Isaac Newton saw an expanded theory of gravity. A torsion spring fell from a worktable and a Naval officer saw more than a clumsy spill. Richard James saw a Slinky. A rubber compound spilled onto a tennis shoe and a chemist saw more than a stubborn stain. Patsy Sherman saw Scotchgard, a spill to protect against all spills. A moldy culture of bacteria sat forgotten in a laboratory, yet a scientist saw more than dirty equipment. Alexander Fleming saw penicillin."[11]

Llopis goes on to tell the story of the Swiss electrical engineer George de Mestral, who went on a daylong hunting trip with his dog in 1941. When he returned home after the day in the foothills of the Alps, he noticed dozens of burrs stuck to his wool pants. They sparked a childlike curiosity. He pulled one free and observed it under a microscope. He noticed the burr had tiny hooklike arms that allowed it to grab the tiny loops of fabric on his pants. An idea was born, but not just any idea—one that would lead to the creation of a multimillion-dollar company.

The idea: Velcro.

It's one of those creations, like the hanger or the paper clip, that seems so simple we could have thought of it ourselves. It is usually true. We could have come up with the idea, maybe even should have—but only if we had allowed space in our often stringent schedules and blinkered mind for spontaneous creativity. As a child, you had only two things on your calendar, and both of them could occur at any moment of any hour: exploration and creation. Rescheduling wasn't an option. It was now. Or it was never.

4. Play Is the Supreme Catalyst

Of play, author Jack Uldrich writes, "It allows people to practice skills they might need later down the line. But play goes beyond such life skills. When we play, we gain practice manipulating things and controlling the outcome of events. We also devise new solutions for old problems and create new endings for our experiences."[12]

The inimitable British essayist G. K. Chesterton wrote, "The true object of all human life is play." It wasn't just an offhanded mention. Chesterton wrote many essays and books on various themes but none more than the subject of play. *Manalive* is a case in point. The title alone reveals its thrust, but the story itself is anything but predictable. It is the story of Innocent Smith, a man who is either completely mad or the most brilliant one of all. He blows onto the scene of a dull and lifeless London boardinghouse on the wings of a great windstorm, wearing a tight green suit. To say he is eccentric is an understatement. He is so vivacious and full of antics that few know what to do with him. But they are drawn to his sweet nature nonetheless. Soon Smith's presence reverses the mood of the dreary boardinghouse. A once hesitant Inglewood confesses his love for Diana Duke, the landlady's niece. A cynical journalist named Michael makes amends with the heiress Rosamund Hunt. And Smith himself makes secret plans to elope with the heiress's paid companion, Mary Gray. All seems perfect—until two doctors appear with the news that Innocent Smith is wanted on charges of burglary, bigamy, and attempted murder. Smith pulls a revolver and, seemingly confirming the charges, shoots twice at one of the doctors, narrowly missing his head.

Smith is subsequently tried, but in an unexpected twist all evidence points to his being, like his name, innocent of all charges or, as Chesterton puts it, "blameless as a buttercup." In a masterful conclusion, the truth is revealed: Innocent Smith shot at people to inspire them to value their lives; the house he broke into was his own; and the women he allegedly had an affair with were all the same woman—his wife masking her identity with aliases so they could continually reenact their courtship.

Innocent Smith would be a welcomed addition to many homes and offices I know. He is a fictitious, childlike character that represents that missing element in so many adult lives. But the point is not that we need him. The point is that we can be him. We can enter the office with more pep in our step, a curious smirk, an eager expectation that any workday can be a great adventure if we know how to think and where to look.

At one point we all were as playful as Innocent Smith.

This is not just an unsupported hypothesis, as author Jack Uldrich points out. "Play has consistently been found to reduce stress, increase energy levels, brighten people's outlook, increase optimism and foster creativity."[13]

A rediscovery is in order. No, a *resurrection*. A resurrection of the manner in which you used to live out your days. A resurrection of the person you used to be. "Life is a hypocrite," wrote British playwright Christopher Fry, "if I can't live the way it moves me."[14] It's time to live as you are moved to live. With passion. Curiosity. Freedom.

"Play without keeping score," writes Roy Williams, founder of the Wizard Academy in Austin, Texas. "Play requires the relaxation of the uptight mind. We are rejuvenated and revitalized by it. Children are happy because they play. Adults are unhappy because they do not."[15]

When we were children, despite the circumstances surrounding us, despite our lack of skills and tangible resources, life still burst forth with possibility at every turn. In that context, creativity flowed wildly and continuously. We lived by the rhythms in our hearts and in the world around us. We fearlessly followed the paths of curiosity before us, wherever they might lead. We did this every day.

But that was then. Somewhere, somehow, our innocent, hypercreative life began to give way to another less wild and less wondrous existence. The easy explanation is that we grew up. It's only part of the story.

NOW . . .
(who you are)

what is left of you

> *Too many people grow up. That's the real*
> *trouble with the world, too many people grow*
> *up. They forget. They don't remember what*
> *it's like to be twelve years old.*
>
> —WALT DISNEY

"Life is either a daring adventure," said Helen Keller, "or it is nothing." Follow a random sampling of American business professionals for a week and you might conclude that the latter half of Keller's quote is the bane of adult existence. Life is not a daring adventure, especially not at work. And while our lives at home might not be as bad, spending the majority of our waking hours on nothing is tragic. "Ambition called to me," laments the poet Edgar Lee Masters, "but I dreaded the chances. Yet all the while I hungered for meaning in my life."[1]

What has become of that unbridled sense of wonder, adventure, and creativity we used to own? Most would say you and I just grew up. It's a shallow explanation, especially if we are being honest with ourselves.

Are your days truly exhilarating? Or, as Masters poetically confesses, is there something you still hunger for all the while?

There is a phenomenon in the medical world called "phantom pain." It's the sensation of pain in a limb that is no longer a part of a person's body. It is most common in patients who have had an arm or a leg amputated, but it also occurs in women after mastectomy or in patients who've had an internal organ removed. The hunger for creativity you feel as an adult is a lot like phantom pain. The only difference is that the part of you that's missing is actually still there. It's just been paralyzed since childhood.

Life is most vivid when it is dynamic. Yet it becomes, for most of us, an exercise in maintaining homeostasis. This tack is safe, yes. And strategic. Even constant and reliable. Yet ultimately we end up living Groundhog Days without the initiative or ingenuity to make them better. The creative path began fading somewhere during our elementary schooling, and as we grew older it eventually faded out of sight.

"Modern learning has done us a disservice," writes Debra Jennings of Project Smart. "From Kindergarten on, we've been taught to learn with primarily one side of our brain, the left one, where analytical skills, facts, rational thought and logic are housed. Primary schools with shrinking budgets have focused their efforts on reading, writing and arithmetic, cutting superfluous classes in art, music and physical education. Even the SAT exam has traditionally focused on left-brained verbal skills and math."[2]

As you advanced further in school you were less encouraged and rewarded for abstract, artsy thinking. The value of art was increasingly ignored or at best relegated to non-compulsory status. Artists were a small band of outsiders. Insiders were placed on an education track in which you were praised for parroting information in preexisting, predefined answers—for using logic and memory rather than imagination and creativity. There was increasingly less credence given to the whys, what ifs, and maybes that once flowed from your being.

The working world then fell right in step. You were given a script for productivity and rewarded for remaining in the system. This only reinforced the static mode of operation you'd been taught for a dozen or more years in school.

If that wasn't bad enough, your education and corporate environment weren't the only forces at work against your creative side. As you grew up, the half of your brain that neurologists call your "left hemisphere" began to dominate your thinking. This is the part of you that thrives off logic, predictability, and concrete definition. It aims to make perfect sense of the world around you and, in theory, make decisions more efficient and life more safe and manageable.

"As we grow older, certain behaviors naturally abate," explains Alison Gopnik, a professor of psychology and affiliate professor of philosophy at Berkeley. "While we're all glad our days of thumb-sucking and bed-wetting are behind us, positive traits such as limitless imagination and spontaneity also diminish. . . . Our ability to learn new things is another primary positive characteristic we lose over time."[3]

Gopnik offers a computer science metaphor that explains the divergence that occurs between our perception as children and our perception as adults. There are two types of computer systems: those that "explore," taking in any and all information that might be relevant; and those that "exploit," taking in only the information that is relevant for their goals.

As children we were an exploring system, taking it all in to see what might result. We learned like crazy via the constant collision of new pieces of information. Possibilities were endless. Creativity came easy. But as we grew into adults we morphed into an exploiting system that picked and chose intake on a need-to-know basis.

The problem with an exploiting system is that we can get indefinitely bogged down in the opinions and conclusions we've already formed. Typically the longer we live as adults, the more inflexible those conclusions are and the more difficult it becomes for us to see and seize new possibilities. There is a phrase we use to describe a person in this state: he is "stuck in his ways." The truth is that as predominantly left-brained adults we are all stuck in our ways of perceiving information. Along the road from childhood to adulthood, we steadily lost the need for imagination and exploration to help formulate answers to our questions. We learned instead to rely on what we already knew to make decisions, offer explanations, and solve problems. Efficiency became our vehicle for progress, replacing curiosity.

In 2005, a study co-conducted by Vladimir Sloutsky, professor and director of the Center for Cognitive Science at Ohio State University, and Anna Fisher, a graduate student at Ohio State, showed that adults were better at remembering pictures of imaginary animals they had seen only once than they were at remembering pictures of real cats they'd seen all their lives.[4] The results point to the decline in mental functionality that occurs as we increase in knowledge. Sometimes what we know just gets in the way. In such cases, say Sloutsky and Fisher, we are far better off approaching a subject with a childlike sense of naïveté.

"Verbatim memory is often a property of being a novice," explains Sloutsky. "As people become smarter, they start to put things into categories, and one of the costs they pay is lower memory accuracy for individual differences." In other words, we fail to see the very details that not only spark new thoughts and better conclusions but also give color to an otherwise monochrome perspective.

Sloutsky and Fisher's study also included a test in which five-, seven-, and eleven-year-old children and college-age adults were asked to view a picture of a cat, which they were told had "beta cells inside its body." The groups were then shown thirty pictures of other animals (cats, bears, and birds) and asked whether each animal had beta cells in its body. Afterward, the participants were reminded that only cats had beta cells in their bodies.

Finally, the participants were shown twenty-eight more pictures of animals and asked to identify which ones had been shown previously. The results showed that the five-year-olds were the most accurate at remembering which animals they had seen before. The seven-year-olds were second best, and the eleven-year-olds were third best. The adults were the worst at recalling which animals they had seen.

Sloutsky explained that the reason the younger children— especially the five-year-olds—were far better than the adults in the test was that they had not yet learned to categorize the animals in their minds. As a result, they studied each picture closely to determine whether it was similar to the one of the cat who had beta cells. On the other hand, once the adults learned that only the cat had beta cells, they no longer paid attention to the details of any other pictures. The cat pictures were the only ones that mattered to them. If it wasn't a picture of a cat, it was insignificant.

In his conclusion, Sloutsky pointed to an inverse relationship between our propensity to categorize as adults and our ability to recognize distinctions as children. It seems that when we categorize we lose sight of details. And when we focus in on details, we lose sight of categories.

The truth is that we need both abilities as working adults.

We need to be able to know when one subject is highly relevant and when another is irrelevant to a particular task. We need to possess the ability to be highly efficient at times.

We also need to possess the ability to be inefficient and forget categories in an effort to solve a difficult problem, create a breakthrough product, or come up with a new way of doing things. The irony is that in times like these inefficiency is more effective, and efficient, than efficiency.

Yet most of us find ourselves stuck in the mode of efficiency. We try to solve problems and originate ideas within the bubble of our current knowledge and experience. Our felt needs are telltale signs of this inclination.

We just need more time. More energy. Better resources—a new job, a better position, a bigger budget, more income. We think these external factors are the key to a breakthrough. We treat them like shoes; if we can just find the right fit, we will finally hit full stride and be both successful and satisfied.

It's a lost cause. The greatest resource we have is not external. It's creativity. It's our internal resourcefulness—our ability to differentiate, reformulate, and adapt to our ever-changing circumstances. Our ability to use circumstances to our advantage. Such resourcefulness is not a function of the current resources of your left brain. Such resourcefulness requires abstract thinking—new considerations and collisions of thought; an anarchical approach to all you currently know or thought you knew.

With our efficient left brains in charge, our best-case scenario is that we become impassive productivity machines, sustained by the biweekly fuel of a paycheck and kept hopeful by the false promise of "someday." Someday I'll have all the tools and the time I need to get it right. Someday I'll do that. Someday I'll visit there again. Someday I'll take that back up. Someday I'll slow down and have the time. Someday . . .

Pursuing someday is no way to live.

While your left brain is a critical part of your existence because it is ultimately what protects you from touching the hot stove or ramming the car that just cut you off, your left brain alone leaves your creativity handcuffed and your life effectively colorless. You work harder and smarter but within the mathematical context of logic and reason. The equation goes like this: Work = Pay; Hard Work = Higher Pay; Smart Work + Hard Work = Higher Pay Sooner. The problem is that "higher pay sooner" doesn't truly satisfy anyone who still has to work hard and smart at a job marked by routine and boredom. The real problem or boredom still remains. And you haven't reached any new level of problem solving.

Even when companies attempt to bring off-the-job joys

into the workplace with amenities like onsite gyms, child care, and spa treatments, the real problem still remains. Such things don't make your work itself any more inspiring. They just numb the pain a little while you're there.

The other unfortunate result of a left-brain operating mode is a narrow definition of art that includes only Picasso paintings and Hemingway novels rather than the activity that will unlock breakthrough levels of thinking, performance, and satisfaction. Today, you no longer raise your hand when asked if you are an artist because, clearly, you are not Picasso. But you truly can be in your own way.

The part of you that effervesced creativity as a child is still there. You can stuff it, ignore it, even talk yourself out of it. But every so often, your artist's voice will still whisper to you. Through a vibrant sunset. An inspiring film. The birth of a child. A poignant tragedy. The whispers are both subtle and sharp reminders of what is still inside you scratching to come back out and play.

Consider the results of a 2009 study conducted by the psychology department at North Dakota State University titled "Child's Play: Facilitating the Originality of Creative Output by a Priming Manipulation." Scientists within the department took a large group of randomly selected undergraduates and separated them into two groups. The first group was given the following instruction: "You are seven years old. School is cancelled, and you have the entire day to yourself. What would you do? Where would you go? Who would you see?"

The second group was given the same instructions, minus "You are seven years old." The students wrote for ten minutes and were then given a version of the Torrance Test of Creative Thinking, which included tasks like completing unfinished drawings or inventing ways to repurpose a used item.

The first group, who imagined themselves as seven-year-olds, scored much higher.

While a conclusion like "Think like a seven-year-old to reclaim your creativity" seems reasonable, it can be misleading, says creativity consultant and *Psychology Today* blogger Jeffrey Davis. He cites Pulitzer Prize winner Ellen Gilchrist, who, while watching her three-year-old grandchild, mused, "How to hold onto that genius?" and nineteenth-century poet Charles Baudelaire, who once wrote, "Genius is the capacity to retrieve childhood at will," as examples in a long line of the same sort of thinking. But, says Davis, while it's true that "infants, toddlers, and children have a perpetual fascination with all-things-new . . . that we adults often sorely lack . . . highly creative people are not retrieving childhood—which includes, remember, all of its muddled-ness and meanness and necessary dependency and utter self-centeredness. These adults are retrieving wonder."[5]

Davis suggests a new way of thinking about reclaiming our creative genius that was so prevalent in childhood. Instead of claiming, as Baudelaire did, that "genius is the capacity to retrieve childhood at will," we should say, "Genius is the capacity to retrieve *wonder* at will." This way, Davis says, "We're not nostalgically trying to bring back some 'lost child' or 'find our inner child.' We are supremely present with who and how we are."

What you need to know—what perhaps no one has ever told you—is that an artist is anyone who challenges conventional wisdom and inspires change that creates new channels of problem solving and innovation. And art is much broader and more accessible than a priceless masterpiece painted centuries ago. Art is not only a noun; it is a verb. It is not only a canvas; it is a catalyst. Art is far less about the physical thing created than about the effect of your ideas, words, and creations on your circumstances and the others around you.

The truth is that regardless of your age or perceived artistic skills, you can be an artist with a unique ability to create meaningful, breakthrough art on a regular basis, no matter where you work and no matter what your job title happens to be.

The trick is to begin seeing yourself that way—the way you once did. It may feel like standing on your head at first, but that's okay. Sometimes we need a little rush to shake us from our slumber.

The brilliant Russian writer Leo Tolstoy had a way of turning things on their heads to open up readers' minds to a perspective they had never considered before. He described boredom as "the desire for desires." How true it is that even being bored proves we still have something left inside that's itching to get out. Don't ignore the itch any longer. It's the door to your fearless creativity, the path to rediscovering your days as the adventure they truly are—opportunities for new solutions you hadn't considered and greater successes you hadn't imagined. "To put meaning in one's life may end in madness," concludes Edgar Lee Masters in *Spoon River*

Anthology, "but life without meaning is the torture of rest-lessness and vague desire—it is a boat longing for the sea and yet afraid."[6]

Resurrecting your artist inside begins by awakening to what is true about you right now. "I am not a mechanism," wrote D. H. Lawrence. And neither are you. You are more than a yes-man or yes-woman capable of producing only pre-programmed answers and predetermined solutions. You may have been acting like that for such a long time that it seems absurd to think you could actually do something different, something truly artistic, truly creative, eccentric, and adventurous. But there is no question you can. The real question is: Will you?

Years ago a North Face ad campaign punched the business world in the gut.

"I am not alive in an office," it began. "I am not alive in a taxi cab. I am not alive on a sidewalk . . ."

The punch line?

"Never stop exploring."

That's my challenge to you right now. "We shall not cease from exploration," wrote T. S. Eliot, "and the end of all our exploring will be to arrive where we started and know the place for the first time." You may have stopped exploring for a season—even a long season. But you can start again now and never stop again.

The misconception many have is that we must go out in order to find that place—to the woods or the mountains or another country on a long sabbatical. While wild and new places certainly have a way of reminding us of the fullness of our potential, the truth is that we can find a wild and new place anywhere if we tap into our inner artist. Even at your workplace.

In 2005, author Daniel Pink wrote, "The future belongs to a very different kind of person with a very different kind of mind." According to him, "The era of left-brain domi-nance, and the information age that it engendered, is giving way to a new world in which creative and holistic right-brain abilities mark the fault line between who gets ahead and who falls behind."[7]

That future is here. And that very different kind of person with a very different kind of mind is the artist. But not just any artist, and certainly not the artists I met early on in my journey to rediscovering my fearless creativity—those with incredible skills but without strategic sense enough to make their art meaningful to others in the world. No, the artist I'm talking about—that Daniel Pink was talking about—is the one who knows when to embrace the childlike creativity of the right brain and when to embrace the logical strategy of the left brain. It's a potent combination. And best of all, it's who you truly are when you are whole.

Here's how.

HOW . . .
(who you can still be)

3

be provocative

Loyalty to petrified opinions never yet broke a chain or freed a human soul in this world—and never will.

—MARK TWAIN

"If John Lennon had only been one of the four members of the Beatles, his artistic immortality would already have been assured."[1] So begins John Lennon's biographic description on the website dedicated to his memory. There is no doubt Lennon was a music icon. You could even argue that his solo success after the Beatles is proof that his lyrical genius would have won him acclaim apart from his association with the world-famous band. He was a man of indisputable talent. But it was not his ability to write or sing a song that set him apart. It was his ability to provoke the hearts and minds of the world that made him such a singularly memorable artist. He is a model for those of us who want our best work to stand out and have the impact it truly can.

While many have come to know Lennon as a symbol of peace, it was actually his outspoken nature that brought him much of the attention and notoriety he had throughout his life. His observation that the Beatles were "more popular than Jesus" compelled many listeners to burn the band's albums and many U.S. radio stations to cease playing their songs. Later, his denunciation of America's involvement in the Vietnam War and his subsequent activism throughout the 1960s and '70s put him at odds with millions abroad. But it also led millions to hold him up as an icon of a growing countercultural sentiment. Make love, not war. Give peace a chance. "Imagine," he sang, ". . . someday you'll join us, and the world will live as one."

Yes, John Lennon was a skilled musician. But iconic status as an artist then and now is not the result of the mere notes he placed on a page. It is the result of being provocative.

John Lennon was, and still is, a polarizing figure: a model citizen to some, a model threat to others. Despite what you thought about John Lennon, it was impossible to ignore him. He was a dreamer who didn't keep his dreams to himself. He was courageous enough to provoke those around him to imagine a better life, whether or not they agreed with his notions of how. But what is often lost in the debate on his life is that, ultimately, John Lennon wanted little more than you or I want. "When I went to school," he once explained, "they asked me what I wanted to be when I grew up. I wrote down 'happy.' They told me I didn't understand the assignment, and I told them they didn't understand life."

The only difference between Lennon and the average person is that he was willing to do something about his pursuit of happiness rather than let circumstances dictate life for him. It sometimes involved rattling the cages around long-standing beliefs and institutions. That is what made him a memorable artist. And that is what will elevate you and your work to their true potential—if you are willing to rattle some cages too, including your own.

CONTROLLING THE CONTROLLABLE

Look around. Is anything truly reliable? Weather patterns surprise us. New people pop into our lives and old friends disappear. Markets shift without warning. Competition rises up when we least expect it. What works well today might not work at all tomorrow. What we know today could be dead wrong tomorrow. We've all experienced this time and again. "The Universe is change," wrote the ancient Roman emperor Marcus Aurelius in *Meditations*. He is right. Change is the most consistent thread in our circumstances. Despite our concerted efforts at clarity and stability, uncertainty and instability remain.

They attack from outside forces we did not expect and cannot control. They also arise from inside forces we had forgotten or had not yet realized were there—think of the changes that occur when you fall in love or discover a new-found passion.

Some people wait until they are provoked by these forces to change, until their cages are rattled for them and their hand is forced. Artists don't wait to be rattled only from the outside. They provoke themselves first, and then the people around them, in order to constantly imagine new possibilities. They instigate change even when it doesn't seem necessary.

No great and necessary change has come without this sort of provocation.

From Joan of Arc, Luther, and Wilberforce to Gandhi, King, and Mandela, many of history's greatest leaders were simply common people who were compelled to provoke us to think and act differently, not in a contrived effort at vainglory but because something about their circumstances demanded a better way. They were provocative because they lived with conviction that life itself could and should continually advance toward a higher standard and produce a more fulfilling result.

On resisting England's imperialism in France, the teen-aged peasant girl Joan of Arc asserted, "To sacrifice what you are and to live without belief, that is a fate more terrible than dying."

When threatened with arrest and urged to recant his Ninety-Five Theses indicting the Roman Catholic Church of ungodly behavior, the German monk Martin Luther held firm, responding, "Here I stand, I cannot do otherwise."

In response to harsh criticism of his antislavery campaign in England, the statesman William Wilberforce proclaimed, "If to be feelingly alive to the sufferings of my fellow-creatures is to be a fanatic, I am one of the most incurable fanatics ever permitted to be at large."

An impoverished but no less determined Mahatma Gandhi maintained, "A 'No' uttered from the deepest conviction is better than a 'Yes' merely uttered to please, or worse, to avoid trouble."

The man who provoked America toward racial equality,

Martin Luther King Jr., declared, "A man who won't die for something is not fit to live."

And the leader who became a prisoner to free his country from bigotry, Nelson Mandela, avowed, "There is no passion to be found playing small."

While history does not categorize them as artists, all were artists of the highest form. Their brushes and paints were the words and actions that pointed to the better way and the higher standard. Their canvas was the inert culture in which they lived. Their art was the positive change they eventually brought about.

They were artists not because they produced a piece of music or a colored canvas to entertain the masses. They were artists because they had the courage to challenge the flawed and unsatisfactory mores of their day and take ground-breaking action to improve them.

While the results of their art changed the course of history, the nature of their circumstances is not unfamiliar to you or me. All found themselves in the midst of conditions that were not all they could or should be. While they could not change the history that brought about the deficiencies, they could control the way forward as much as one individual was able, which is more than many of us realize. All believed they had a say in the solution. And they did something you and I can do anytime we are faced with a challenge or problem. They provoked themselves and others to find the solution rather than sitting idly by and hoping for it to arrive by happenstance.

» «

The prevailing systems in which you live and work are largely unquestioned. This is often most true at work, where you are given a position and a list of responsibilities and then trained in the best practices for producing results. What say do you have in that? Very little, other than the degree to which you embrace the system. Things tend to run themselves at work, and the unspoken sentiment is that you don't fix what isn't broken. This cycle promotes a stale and lifeless existence. There is a reason corporations are called "machines." It's the same reason many jobs are so dissatisfying. We tend to accept an unsatisfactory existence as a necessary evil. That's just part of growing up and working in the real world, we tell ourselves. You can't get everything you want, we say, as if it were pointless to wish things were better. And so we eventually reach a point where we just unquestioningly plug into the systems around us and do our jobs like ants in a colony, no questions asked.

Don't get me wrong. There is nothing wrong with a best-practices strategy. Creating and sustaining a system that produces predictable results is necessary—especially in business. Where a company runs into trouble is when its people aren't trained to think beyond how things have always been done and a system starts failing to produce the needed results. And this always happens, by the way, because there are things no business can control.

No matter what position you hold in a company, you cannot control the economy. You cannot forecast the moves of your competition. You cannot predict global patterns or how they will affect your buyers' habits. Even if you've done your homework, you can't foresee customers' reactions with 100 percent accuracy. With unavoidable uncertainty on the horizon, the best thing you can do is put yourself in a better position for when conditions do change—because they will. That's where being a provocative employee becomes a great advantage to any company.

BECOMING INDISPENSABLE

By becoming provocative—by constantly looking for obstacles to growth and opportunities for progress regardless of your daily duties—you can provide your company with a measure of critical preparation it doesn't currently have. In doing so, not only will you bolster your value to the organization, but you will open your job up to new frontiers.

When I spoke to a group of Microsoft employees in 2008, Fred Jordan was in the audience. His department had recently been tasked with the job of reducing the cost of the goods that Microsoft sold. At the time, most Microsoft goods consisted of software delivered on CDs and DVDs. The evening after my performance, Fred boarded a plane for New York to join his team for more formal meetings that surrounded solving this latest business challenge. The team came up with a couple of ideas they would follow up on once back at the office, but both Fred and everyone else knew the ideas weren't groundbreaking.

While back at the airport, awaiting his return flight home to Seattle, Fred had a couple of drinks at the bar as the challenge weighed heavily on his mind. He mulled things over again and again. Once airborne, he took out a pad of paper and drew a typical flowchart with Microsoft at the top of the page symbolized by a large circle and then several lines reaching down to several smaller circles, which represented their biggest buyers. He stared at it for a few moments and then started jotting down anything that came to mind:

- Reduce the cost of manufacturing CDs and DVDs.
- Reduce the cost of the software packaging.
- Reduce the cost of shipping the CDs and DVDs.

It was all underwhelming, and frankly nothing his department hadn't already explored. He was running up against the same wall. It seemed they'd already reduced the cost of the software as much as possible. Was there something he was missing? An element in the transaction he hadn't considered?

He stared at the drawing again and that's when he recalled something very simple I had suggested at my event to provoke creativity. I encouraged the audience to begin viewing their problems from a different perspective. This is when Fred's breakthrough idea began coming into focus.

He picked up the pad of paper and flipped it upside down so that the buyers of Microsoft software were now at the top of the page. What if he began to see this as not merely Microsoft's problem to solve but that of the buyers as well? He began wondering what they might have said if they had been tasked with the same challenge of reducing costs. What did they truly care about? What didn't really matter to them at all?

That's when it hit him. What the buyers cared about was

not what he had been exploring. They cared primarily about receiving the software in a timely fashion. And they cared about the software working properly. The methods of manufacturing and packaging weren't really on their radar as long as they promptly got what they paid for and it performed as expected. With his buyers' viewpoint, and with the confidence that the software already performed well, Fred wondered if there was a way to make the entire process about better delivery in a way that would benefit everyone in the value chain.

The lightbulb popped on. Digital by Choice was born—a program that would give buyers the opportunity to receive their Microsoft software by digital delivery instead of CDs or DVDs, thus reducing costs of production, increasing speed of delivery, and reducing the carbon footprint of the entire transaction. Keep in mind this was at a time when software companies still delivered the vast majority of their products on disks. The idea of digital delivery was not the status quo. CDs and DVDs were, and that's what everyone expected. But there was a better, cheaper, more eco-friendly way that no one had thought to consider on such a large scale. Until Fred Jordan did.

In the weeks that followed, Microsoft team members created the Digital by Choice website, where customers could choose digital delivery and accomplish three things: (1) faster access to purchased software and immediate access to new updates; (2) the elimination of the receipt, cataloguing, distribution, and disposal of disks; and (3) a reduction in their carbon footprint through a reduction in the need to manufacture, ship, and ultimately dispose of disks.[2] The team then began to alert buyers of this opportunity. The results were huge.

While I have been asked by Microsoft, a tremendously savvy competitor, to not share the financial specifics of the money they saved that same year, I can say that adoption of Digital by Choice was immediate and widespread, and the first-year savings totaled an amount so jaw-dropping that Fred won the prestigious Microsoft Circle of Excellence Award at the end of 2008, and was subsequently given a promotion and a team of his own to continue provoking significant progress for Microsoft and its constituents. That is what an employee who is willing to provoke the status quo can do for a company. That is also what provoking the status quo can do for your career.

The truth is that most companies need creativity more than they need clarity or stability. Most people in most companies aren't provocative because homeostasis is held to be the Holy Grail. If everyone just does his and her job, the system will work itself. We'll all be secure and make our money . . . and unicorns will prance at our Christmas party. It doesn't work in today's chaotic and rapid-fire digital world.

Business systems often work in opposition to your maximum potential because in reality they give you and everyone else in the company an overconfident sense of stability. The "don't rock the boat" sentiment that arises from this sense discourages you from bringing your best effort.

Ignore the sentiment.

Rock the boat.

It's what the best businesses really want. In 2010, IBM revealed their findings from a survey in which they asked chief executives to name the most crucial factor for future successes. From in-person interviews with more than 1,500 CEOs from sixty countries and thirty-three industries worldwide, IBM reported, "Chief executives believe that—more than rigor, management discipline, integrity or even vision—successfully navigating an increasingly complex world will require creativity." Yet the same study also revealed that "less than half of global CEOs believe their enterprises are adequately prepared" for the future.[3]

Why are so many companies unprepared?

Because necessity is the mother of invention, and most companies don't view creativity as a necessity until they are desperate for it. That's where you come in.

The chief execs IBM surveyed were also asked to name the activities that would define successful creative leaders in the future. Creative leaders, they responded,

- invite disruptive innovation, invite others to drop outdated approaches and take balanced risks
- consider previously unheard-of ways to drastically change the enterprise for the better
- are comfortable with ambiguity and experiment to create new business models
- are courageous enough to make decisions that alter the status quo
- will invent new business models based on entirely different assumptions.[4]

In sum, the future belongs to those who are provocative enough to rock the boat not just now and then but on a regular basis. It's the only way your company will remain nimble enough to respond to crises and maintain a level of innovation that will keep it growing. Few have understood this better than Soichiro Honda, the founder of the Japanese car company that bears his name.

Honda personally experienced numerous crises and unexpected setbacks in his early years in the auto industry. His factory was once destroyed by fire. His supplies were rationed during wartime. Designs failed and threw production schedules into a panic. While the crises weren't welcomed, Honda began to note how each crisis improved the eventual outcome. Ironically, the trials often sharpened his workers and left his company with better results than if everything had gone as scripted. For example, it took a steel shortage for him to discover that aluminum not only made lighter engine blocks but also dissipated heat better. A design failure that seemed catastrophic turned out to be the doorway to a landmark innovation.

Over time Soichiro Honda came to value uncertainty as a catalyst for breakthroughs—so much so that he implemented a management practice that became known as "kick out the ladder." Just as a team neared completion on a project, he would create a crisis that seemed to threaten everything. He would then shorten the deadline. Each time he kicked the ladder out from under his people, they were forced to improvise. They stopped relying on "what we've done before" and shifted into a hypercreative gear. Their resulting work improved. Some of Honda's most important developments over the years were fueled by this purposeful provocation. There is a critical lesson here for you and the company you work for.

Without exception, progress comes as a result of change. At times a small change can be a catalyst for great results. At other times, a bigger change, a full-scale change, is required to get us out of a "don't rock the boat" rut. Either way, we have a choice to make. We can wait for that catalyst to come to us and then struggle to find a solution on the fly with rusty tools. Or we can originate the catalysts ourselves and begin developing a creative reflex when an account or our jobs aren't on the line, so that when they are, coming through in innovative fashion is second nature.

In theater improv, this technique is called "raising the stakes." On stage, an actor will throw an unexpected twist into the plot that changes the circumstances in the scene, escalating the drama. When a scene goes from "Someone is at the door" to "The FBI is at the door with a search warrant," the stakes change. The other actors on stage are forced to create new, unscripted reactions. The scene is heightened and it becomes more captivating. The sudden shifts provoke fresh thinking and, more important, fresh possibilities. With practice, improv actors are masters at creating on the fly in any scenario. It is because they are willing to be provocative and be provoked.

The truth is that you probably experience this "raising the stakes" phenomenon often without being aware of it. It happens in everyday life when various circumstances force you out of your comfort zone. Roy Williams, former acclaimed radio ad writer and the founder of the Wizard Academy, once mentioned to his longtime friend, a psychologist, that he always had his best ideas on the plane rides home after speaking engagements. "Well of course," his friend replied. "Working to connect to an audience is an extroverted feeling, your least preferred function." When the friend saw Williams was confused, he explained, "Psychologists have known for years that a person's fourth function—the one least preferred—is the trap door to the unconscious mind." Essentially Williams was his most creative when the creative part of his mind that was not aware of his rules and systems had been unlocked by an uncomfortable situation. This led Williams to conclude that "humans are like neon; we glow when we release the energy of overstimulation."[5]

While nearly everyone has experienced a "spark" of creativity before, most can't call it up at will. Even fewer live in a constant state of creativity. But those who do are the game changers.

There is no doubt that formal training in your position is valuable. You must have specific know-how to be an accurate accountant, or a helpful customer service rep, or an effective salesperson. But in those crucial moments when everything must come together, when you're making decisions on the fly and solving problems in real time, it's your talent at improvising that governs your performance. When you learn to be provocative every day, creativity is always accessible. Breakthroughs are far more common.

Despite all the planning and forecasting involved in running a company or your career, lasting progress hinges on your ability to provoke positive adjustments before they are desperately needed. Progress from passive change is perilous;

it requires faith in factors you cannot control. It's like being in a rowboat on the open sea. When the waters are calm you get a deceptive sense of control with those oars. You can move in any direction with a little effort. It's only when the wind starts rising and the swells stretch to twenty feet that you realize how small those oars—and your hard work—really are. If you don't have an engine on that boat, you're headed wherever the wind and waves take you.

When you are on the open sea—and you are in nearly every business profession on the planet—an engine will not only keep you ahead of the storm but help you survive the storms you cannot avoid. That engine is your ability to provoke change.

Sustained progress comes from the ability to (1) provoke the change that is necessary before your hands are tied, and (2) provide the innovation necessary to avoid ruts in progress and fulfillment. This is as true for your individual career as it is for the company you work for. Being provocative can protect you from job stagnation. It can protect you from becoming a dispensable employee. It can protect you from deception among the ranks or worse, staying on a sinking ship. It can also ensure that the work you do every day is more than dutiful and dogmatic. It can bring your work and your workplace to life. But only if you are willing to invite it in even when the waters are smooth.

Being provocative is the essence of what Gandhi meant when he famously asserted, "Be the change you wish to see in the world." Here is how you can start being the change you wish to see in your career, your company, and your world. It is the first mark of a true artist.

ON BEING PROVOCATIVE

"Those who profess to favor freedom," wrote Frederick Douglass, "and yet depreciate agitation, are men who want rain without thunder and lightning." The modern business world wants you to despise disorder despite the reality that progress never occurs without it. Fields never grow green without a regular storm. The natural world is a constant reminder that progress never occurs without some disorder. Here is how to create disorder at work that will inject life into your days and ensure that you and your company remain in a progressive state.

1. Step Outside Your Bubble

Being provocative is ultimately about prodding and questioning the status quo often, and then re-creating the status quo when necessary. This is critical because the status quo does not adjust unless we adjust it. When we don't prod or question the way things are, our existence ends up based on outdated assumptions and erroneous conclusions. Until somebody steps outside the bubble and describes the status quo objectively, as an outsider, it generally doesn't occur to anyone inside the bubble that it's obsolete or even dangerous.

You've probably seen this happen with a friend who remained in a relationship that was nothing she desired. It was obvious to you that the relationship was destined to fail, but your friend remained oblivious. Why? Because she was never able to see with objective eyes what it really was. This impartial self-audit is necessary to rid your work of obstacles to progress. It is also necessary to protect your company and keep it growing.

I'll admit that self-audits are difficult. If I hadn't lost my business, I don't know how long I would have ignored the artist inside me. My self-audit was prompted by my sudden loss, not a regular habit of self-observation. This isn't uncommon. Loss, tragedy, adversity, stress—they each have a way of acting like a refinery, removing all the excess so that only our purest selves remain. But that process is not exactly desirable.

You and I are far better off auditing our circumstances before the rug has been pulled from under us, when we still have greater choice in the matter. In hindsight, it's easy to look back on that difficult time in my life and say it was meant to be. While I am one who believes that things happen for a reason, I'm not one who believes that our fate is predetermined and outside our control. Sure, it's clear now that I am better off being a graffiti artist, but I don't believe I had to come to this discovery by building a business for nearly a decade and then losing it, along with my self-esteem, in a matter of months. If I had been listening to my heart and provoking my circumstances for signs of life—greater satisfaction, deeper meaning, more fun—I would have seen that I needed a change long before my career went into a tailspin.

Despite our desire to see our situations objectively, our emotional attachments and habitual viewpoints often keep us from seeing the key details pointing to a better way. And if we can't audit ourselves, or we just don't trust that we'll see the whole picture objectively, it's also a great idea to allow someone else who is already outside your bubble to offer a fresh pair of eyes on your circumstances. It can be a game changer if you're willing to listen to and trust the observation.

Consider what would happen if a company regularly allowed its people to observe other departments in an effort to always provide their systems and processes with a fresh pair of eyes. Esther Jeles knows the value of this. She's a corporate behavioral specialist with a client list that includes Harpo Entertainment, Leo Burnett, and Chevrolet, among other heavy hitters. She is the one execs call when they have a dispute they can't resolve.

At one point, Jeles received a call in the middle of the night from a top executive who needed her to mediate an impasse that had reached epic proportions. It was just after Hurricane Katrina had devastated the Gulf Coast and surrounding areas. When the tragedy struck, more than three-quarters of this executive's production company—some three hundred employees—had been deployed to the area, with only the instructions to bring back the important stories to be featured on the show. Now two weeks later, employees had trickled back into the office with what they felt were show-worthy stories. The only problem was that each producer and their team thought their story should take precedence. The producers were arguing over priority. Into that mix came the legal department, who were raising red flags about gathering permissions and securing rights before anything was produced at all. They were very concerned that the company not be sued. The producers didn't want to wait—couldn't wait—because the stories were relevant right then. To make matters even worse, no budget had been established for the nearly companywide endeavor. As a result, the total expense had reached six times what the company had spent on any previous production venture. Accounting was throwing their hands into the air as each production executive argued over who should cover which expenses. They were at a loss for how to handle the costs.[6]

Jeles arrived at the company's theater-style meeting room ahead of schedule so she could observe the executives as they entered a few minutes later. As they did, she could see that they each carried a chip on their shoulder. They all had a case to present, and they all felt they were right. Once they'd all taken their seats, Jeles stepped to the front of the room, greeted the crowd, and then asked one of the executive producers to stand up and tell her what his team could have done differently to help the legal department. The spirit of the room immediately changed, and the producer described a few obvious and simple steps his team could have taken to make the attorneys' lives easier.

One by one, Jeles then called on the other team leaders to describe the actions they could have taken to help members of another team. Instead of a tense, bitter battle between headstrong coworkers that would probably not have ended well, the meeting lasted less than thirty minutes as each team of employees realized there was no status quo for the venture and they would need to come together and create a new one that allowed everyone to do their jobs well and allowed the company to continue producing brilliant shows.

After the meeting adjourned, several team leaders stayed behind to brainstorm the way forward together. It was a shocking result considering the circumstances before the meeting. But to Jeles, it was as simple as provoking the employees to step outside their own bubbles and consider their circumstances from a different standpoint. She calls it "louder listening." It made all the difference.

If you are tired of the combative tone in your work meetings, instigate a new tone. At your next opportunity, speak up at the outset and offer some thoughts on how you can be more helpful to another department or more supportive to a coworker. Not only will it provoke your coworkers to reconsider their tone, it will provoke them to consider dropping their agendas and entering into a productive collaboration.

2. Live with Some Discomfort

Often the more discomfort you are able to live with, the more nimble you are in adapting to changing circumstances and seizing ripe opportunities. One of the greatest opportunities for any business today is social media. Yet the process of adoption has been plodding. One reason is that the idea of revealing the humanity behind a brand, the personalities that exist behind the curtain of products, is disturbing to some. Generally, the higher up the hierarchy you go, the greater the discomfort seems to be.

Do executives have more to lose? Is that it? Or do they have more to hide?

It's an interesting question and one that, given some thought, is often answered before a word is spoken, as author and social media guru Amy Jo Martin points out in her book *Renegades Write the Rules*. She describes how in 2010 the most popular sports brand in the world entered into a labor dispute that not only threatened an entire season's worth of revenue but also threatened to damage the brand's public image.[7]

The NFL and the players' association were at a heated impasse over financial terms. In the midst of the debate, the player-representatives were largely outspoken about what they thought and what they were going through. Drew Brees, New Orleans Saints quarterback and one of the NFL's best, was forthright about his opinions and about the progress of the meetings with the NFL executives and owners. The NFL, on the other hand, was silent. Commissioner Roger Goodell's Twitter account went unused for several months.

What do you suppose the message was when Goodell chose to say nothing? Was he strengthening the NFL brand? Was he sending out a good vibe? No, says Martin. Quite the opposite. People assumed he either had something to hide or could ultimately care less about what people thought about him or the brand he represented. His silence was anything but golden. And while it is fairly obvious that people in his position are concerned with saying the wrong thing and jeopardizing the legal process, people in his position are also rarely given such perfect opportunities to bolster a brand's image and connect with the people whose money makes the brand what it is today.

What impact could Goodell have made if he had simply revealed himself to be a real person with honest emotions? At the very least, millions would have understood the pressure of his position better, especially the players whom he had committed to serve. If he were willing to live with some discomfort and reveal a little humanity behind the brand he represents, it is likely many would cut the man some slack.

Don't shy away from discomfort. Enter it, especially if it's a potential door to progress. When I picked up those paint supplies as a suddenly jobless thirty-year-old with three young kids and without enough savings to coast, it was a very uncomfortable move. The left side of my brain was screaming at me to go find a job, any job, before I ran out of money. It was screaming at me to stop screwing around with some ridiculous art form at which I had no experience. But my right brain was telling me otherwise. I knew it was right regardless of the logic that told me it was flippant and dangerous. The truth was that I cared deeply about what I was doing and that the greatest danger lay in going down another wrong path and finding myself stuck in another rut at forty.

Your situation is probably not as dire. But it is no less important. To awaken the artist inside you takes an ability to choose "right" over "want." You will always want comfort and safety. That's in your nature. But progress comes from doing what is right and best and necessary. Confronting a toxic coworker. Pointing out a new problem when the deadline is hours away. Owning a mistake as an individual instead of trying to hide behind "team failure." These are not always comfortable or safe choices, but, then again, we are far more satisfied in an adventure with danger than in no adventure at all.

3. Ask Forgiveness Instead of Permission

This one scares most people. While I'm not suggesting you haul off and pull a stunt that jeopardizes your job, I am en-

couraging you to go with a strong idea whether or not a protocol exists. The reality is that you have a lot more flexibility
in your job than you realize. If you talk on the phone, you
alone control the tone in your voice, the confidence you exude
to people on the other end, and the manner in which you sign
off. While some companies require the same script for greet-
ings and salutations, there are ways to make any script sound
welcoming, and there are ways to make a script sound like a
script. But if you think there is a better way to greet people,
go for it. If it helps constituents connect to you and the company more effectively, I have a good feeling you're not going
to be asked to stop.

Take ownership of your job and elevate it without being
asked and without asking. Do what's best for your work and
your company's success. Earn a reputation for innovation and
excellence in every aspect of what you do. That will only increase the freedom you are given, not jeopardize it.

Tony Hsieh, founder and CEO of the iconic brand Zappos, gives his employees a dangerous degree of freedom in
their interactions with customers. When you come to "Customer Service" in the company handbook, there is only one
rule: "Be yourself and use your best judgment."

That's insane. Guarding the reputation of his company
with "Be yourself"? Letting a multibillion-dollar brand rest
in the "best judgment" of its frontline employees, who are,
coincidentally, also its youngest?

Absolutely. Zappos.com is iconic for this very reason. Its
employees couldn't imagine working anywhere else. They
love their jobs, and they stretch themselves and the rules (in
this case, the one rule) to greater heights of innovation and

execution because they have been entrusted with ownership. The way they shower customers with understanding, commitment, and shocking service—Zappos products have been known to show up at customers' doorsteps in less than twenty-four hours—has earned them a loyal and lucrative following. Do you think Tony Hsieh is wishing he maintained more control? Do you think he stays up at night worrying about ongoing creativity?

Hsieh is a rare leader in an industry—retail—that is known for breakneck systems that leave little room for personal touch. But even if you work within a breakneck system you can push the boundaries. Your choice is simple: either provoke the change you believe is needed or accept the status quo. Often the only time a boss or a company will see the need for change is when the change has been made without permission.

4. Start Small

It might be all that's needed. In 1961, scientist Edward Lorenz was running simulations of the convergence of two weather patterns, using a simple computer model. On one occasion he decided to repeat one of the simulations for a longer period than the first run. He entered the same numeric conditions as those from the first run and then walked away to let the computer do its work.

When he returned, he expected the same results he had seen the first time. Instead, the second weather trajectory diverged from the first on a completely separate path. Lorenz assumed the computer program was malfunctioning.

But upon further observation he realized he had not entered the initial conditions precisely the same as the first time. The computer stored numbers up to six decimal places, like 0.123456, while the printout of the weather results truncated the numbers to only three decimal places, like 0.123. When typing in the second set of conditions, Lorenz had entered the three digit numerals. This small change of less than 0.1 percent altered the result by a significant margin. Though this was a simplified example, Lorenz concluded that predicting weather precisely was impossible.

The following year, Lorenz published a paper on his findings that was largely ignored for a decade. It wasn't until he published another paper in 1972 titled "Does the Flap of a Butterfly's Wings in Brazil Set Off a Tornado in Texas?" that his findings were widely recognized and became known as the "butterfly effect."

The butterfly effect makes an important point about our ability to provoke change in our circumstances. Sometimes all that is needed is a small adjustment to make a major, much-needed impact. An adjustment in schedule. A change in the script. The removal of one step in a process. Often our fear of being provocative is based on the notion that if we speak of or make a change in a process it will be like pulling the office fire alarm. All heads will turn in our direction and the fingers will start pointing. That's almost never the case, especially when you start small. But even if it happens, don't lose sight of the fact that your motive behind provoking positive change is not malicious. It's the opposite. You're aiming for progress, and there will always be those who don't get it and don't like it. Provoke anyway. The world, and your company, needs more provokers. Don't shy away. Don't hold back. Provoking the status quo is the only way anything gets better.

This is the reason I give my paintings away through Art Drops, a Facebook and Twitter treasure hunt in which I hide paintings in random locations in the cities where I am speaking (http://theartofvision.com/artist/art-drops/). I then tweet a clue about the location. If no one finds it, I'll tweet a second clue and post a picture of the painting in its hiding place. The price to play the game is only engagement and the willingness to enter into an adventure. The obvious reward is the painting if you find it. But even if you don't win the painting, the other reward is a break from the typical grind, a reason to get outside and venture out on an adult treasure hunt.

The world is full of artists who sell their paintings on the retail market or through auction houses, but I wanted to push the boundaries on how artwork could affect lives and improve my business. I don't sell art as a commodity; rather, I leverage it as a brand strategy. When people engage with my Art Drops, we are creating relationships and taking a journey together. Not to mention, I am giving someone a free piece of art.

Conventional business wisdom encourages a marketplace of supply and demand. Create. Market. Sell. Profit. I have gone against conventional wisdom to create value that money cannot buy. My higher goal has always been to create an emotional connection or demand for my artwork by not allowing any supply. It's a disruptive strategy.

What does this accomplish?

It raises the value of my work whenever it is available,

for instance, at charitable events. In this way, I am able to use my artwork as a tool to give back and make the world a better place. Last year, at a Hollywood charity event to end domestic violence, celebrity rock star P!nk won my performance painting of Marilyn Monroe with a bid of $10,000. This event was captured by the paparazzi and spread across the celebrity wires around the globe and raised the value of all my paintings overnight.

The other reason I don't follow conventional wisdom in selling my paintings is that I want to make my art available to everyone, not just the über-rich. Art Drops decommoditize my art and make it available to anyone who is willing to engage in the creative process and participate in the treasure hunt. In the end, I profit far more from building an engaged, appreciative following than I would chasing traditional sales revenue. The former is also far more enjoyable.

That's the big secret about being provocative. Not only do you become a change artist in a sea of sameness, you amplify the element of adventure in your own journey. Remember the days when you used to wonder if you could jump from that second stair step? Then one day you did, and all of a sudden a whole new world of flight was possible. In the weeks that followed, you jumped from swings and then the third and fourth step and then the tree branch and then, when the time came, the school's high dive.

Provoking your circumstances works like that. It won't ever be safe—not the first time and not after you've been doing it for a decade. But the more you exercise that muscle, the easier and more exhilarating it becomes. And along the way you'll be reminded again and again that nothing worth achieving ever came without a sacrifice.

Surrender your cozy indifference and jump-start the change that needs to happen. Then do it again and again. There are always things worth fighting for.

be intuitive

> *Big ideas come from the unconscious. This is*
> *true in art, in science, and in advertising. But*
> *your unconscious has to be well informed, or*
> *your idea will be irrelevant. Stuff your conscious*
> *mind with information, then unhook your*
> *rational thought process.*
>
> —David Ogilvy

Whenever I am on tour and have some free time, I try to attend as many local live shows as possible. Whether it's Katy Perry in New Zealand, Korn in London, the Dixie Chicks in Dallas, Rob Bell in Los Angeles, or Deadmau5 in Miami, I attend as a student to better understand the dynamic relationship between different types of performers and their loyal fans. I am a kid again, exploring unknown lands to see what they can tell me about my life and about my work. I don't just sit back in my seat and observe. I aim for full engagement—a full, visceral experience of each show. I am on my feet jumping in unison with the young Deadmau5 crowd or getting bounced around a chaotic mosh pit in front of the Korn stage.

My goal is to understand how and why these performers are successful at connecting with an audience—why do the crowds respond? The answers I find become effective tools when I take the stage for sixty minutes to paint live for a corporate crowd.

After years of using this research method, I've discerned that top performances, though always scripted to some degree, frequently flirt with spontaneity whereby the performer feeds off the crowd and the crowd feeds off the performer. Back and forth like this they go, following each other's lead, prompted by a varying mix of experience and gut instinct. It's systematic know-how grounded by history (as a performer or an attendee) counterbalanced by creative impulse moved by the senses and emotion.

While the top performers I observe certainly plan strategic set lists ahead of time based on what songs their audience enjoys and what sort of show they want to put on, these performers remain keenly aware of the crowd's pulse and know precisely when a departure from the set list is necessary—to thrust the crowd deeper into a trance or lift them higher into a frenzy or usher them into an utter sense of clarity. This ongoing blend of strategy and instinct is a key to navigating the scientific and unscientific nature of our work experience.

There are things we know to be true and things we sense are true. However, the logical side of us wants to lean on only what we know in order to solve our problems and create breakthroughs. Logic tells us that the solution is already available to us based on experience and learnings—it's just a matter of properly rearranging the factors in the equation to find the right answer. This is the main reason careers and companies end up in ruts. What we often call progress is actually just lateral movement within the safe bubble of existing know-how. It's the same product as last year but "new and improved." This applies to the service of customers as well. There's nothing quite so antigroundbreaking as a company's promise to "serve you better." While better versions of the same product are not inherently bad ideas, the products that make the biggest splashes are the first editions, the originals, those that break the mold and create a new opportunity no one thought of before.

These new paths of thought and progress can happen as often as they need to. But first you have to learn to trust more than your current know-how. You have to learn to trust your gut too. The best strategy entails relying, not on one or the other, but on both.

Most of us have problems picking sides. Our educated, corporate brains don't do well with dichotomy. In this case, the dichotomy we struggle with is that of logic and instinct. We typically see them at odds with each other. Either you go with what you know and can predict with a high degree of certainty, or you go out on a limb and hope it holds up. But the truth is that logic—what we know—and instinct—what we sense—can work harmoniously with a little practice.

The artist in you understands this well. As a child you accepted that there were things that you didn't know—things perhaps you might never know—and you plowed forward as though nothing was the matter. Discoveries and breakthroughs were frequent not because you had formulas to predict them but because you had no formulas at all. As a result, resourcefulness was your greatest resource. Your sharpest tools were your senses—you listened for, smelled for, watched for, reached for, and tasted for discoveries that would lead you to knowledge of the world around you. If you've ever been around a toddler, you know that one of your most frequent inquiries was "What's in your mouth?" Legos, rubber bands, Barbie parts, coins, and, unfortunately, even cigarette butts end up being tested for their palatability. A toddler learns quickly what tastes good and what doesn't go well with milk. It seems like an unrefined way to come to conclusions. But it leads to brilliant breakthroughs because no presumptions block the path. As a child, you didn't have enough experience to rule out possibilities before you ran your tests. The truth is that you still don't. You just think you do.

As we said in the previous chapter, because there are so many factors—or forces—outside our control, predicting outcomes is less scientific than we'd like. Lorenz's "butterfly effect" was such a groundbreaking notion because up to that point, meteorologists believed precise weather prediction was attainable. The logic was that once all the variables involved in weather creation were understood completely, one could simply plug the variables into an equation and come out with tomorrow's—and next month's—weather. Lorenz's fortunate accident proved that perfect weather prediction was ultimately a fantasy, especially beyond the next couple of days. Meteorologists could offer educated guesses on the future, but with so many unpredictable variables it was impossible to confidently "know" the outcome. As a result of Lorenz's discovery, meteorologists began developing better reflexes.

Knowing that the future skies could not be scripted, they focused more on reading and reporting the weather over the next twenty-four to seventy-two hours—the period of time that could be "known" with the greatest degree of accuracy because less change could occur in the variables—and being open to seeing signs that they needed to change their predictions.

This is the posture that you and I must take to reclaim our artistic sensibilities at work. There are so many unpredictable variables in our workdays that we can't script creative solutions and continual breakthroughs with data alone. We have to loosen our dependence on what is known so that what is unknown can reach our senses and fuel bigger ideas.

SENSING YOUR WAY

When you were a child you learned so much so fast because knowledge wasn't the Holy Grail of decision making. Discovery was. This imaginative mind-set morphed when you grew up, primarily because the acquisition of knowledge was the only thing you were taught to associate with truth and success. "Knowledge is king" was the message. Ignorance is the enemy.

In the working world the same message holds true. As a result you are not encouraged to explore, to wonder, to theorize. You are encouraged to be certain. While there is undoubtedly a relationship between knowledge and our ability to solve problems and make good decisions, innovation is ultimately limited without intuition. So, therefore, is success.

Regardless of your line of work, you will regularly come across challenges that require more than a solution made up of old data. They will require new thinking. This is when intuition is not only necessary to stay engaged but crucial for igniting the breakthrough that is desperately needed.

A friend recently told me about his experience at an event put on by legendary life coach Tony Robbins. The man whom Larry King once called "the high priest of human potential" is known for the electrifying, enduring energy he's able to get out of a crowd of three-thousand-plus people, typically a mix of Jews, Muslims, and Christians, divorced people, newly-weds, and singles, and both high achievers looking to go higher and those in the lowest of life's lows. From the start of the event at around 8:00 A.M. to the end of the event around midnight or later, there are no formal meal or bathroom breaks. However, every ninety minutes, Robbins cranks up the music and gets everyone on their feet jumping and dancing and having fun. If it sounds a little uncomfortable, that's part of the point. Robbins wants not only to keep you awake and in a peak state so you can truly learn from the experience but to get you outside your comfort zone so you can see new possibilities and perceive your current problems objectively. His heart is to help people see themselves for who they truly can be and then give them the tools to get there. This takes breaking apart the unspoken rules we live by and breaking down the flawed stories we are telling ourselves—then re-creating the correct ones.

For Robbins to accomplish this requires a great deal of intuition about the pulse of the audience. He must know when to take them higher, when to break them down, and when to become something more than a speaker from the stage.

There was a point at his signature "Unleash the Power Within" event that my friend attended where Robbins sensed a need in his audience that would eventually require him to rely on more instinct than knowledge. About six hours into the event, he paused and asked if anyone in the audience thought he or she was suicidal. He explained that in a room full of three thousand people, statistics would say that it was highly likely that a handful would be. This wasn't a time to joke, he asserted. He then asked those who felt they were suicidal to raise their hands.

As my friend looked around, about two dozen had their hands raised in varying degrees of reluctance. Robbins looked at the hands and then stepped down from the stage. Big and muscular at six foot seven, he is typically an imposing presence, but he was anything but imposing in this instance. With the cameras following him and projecting the scene onto two forty-foot screens on each side of the stage, he stepped up to an older man in the front row who appeared to be in his sixties. He asked him to stand and then asked him if he thought he was suicidal. The older man giggled nervously and said he thought so. Robbins asked him why, and the man smiled some more and tried to explain. Robbins smiled and stopped him. He put his arm on the man's shoulder and told him that while he didn't have any doubt he was going through a challenging time, he wasn't suicidal.

Robbins followed a similar protocol with two others in the audience who were having difficult times. Each was enduring challenging circumstances, but none seemed to be truly suicidal. Robbins stepped back on stage and began explaining a lesson about our circumstances and the stories we tell ourselves about our lives and how those stories lead to emotions that dictate the meaningfulness of our lives. And about how often we get the story wrong. My friend said that while the lesson was in context, it was an odd shift, as it seemed Robbins was ignoring the other two dozen or so hands that had gone up. Still the audience was transfixed.

Robbins continued the lesson for a few more minutes, finally explaining the state at which a person truly becomes suicidal. He then paused again and asked for those who thought they were truly suicidal to raise their hands. There was only one.

Robbins looked out over the audience and spotted a good-looking man in his midthirties sitting near the back of the large ballroom. The man's face was blank. Robbins asked the man to stand. Reluctantly, the man did. He was tall and fit and the last person you'd think would be suicidal. As the cameras projected the man's face onto the large screens, Robbins began to ask him general questions about how he felt. The man stared at the foot of the stage as he answered without emotion. Sensing that this was a moment he could not lose, Robbins stepped down from the stage again and walked some seventy-five feet down the right-side aisle until he reached the row where the man was standing, about six rows from the back. He asked the man to come out into the aisle. As the man did, Robbins reached out and gently gripped his shoulder with one hand and pulled him close. With his other hand, Robbins bent his small wire microphone away from his face. With the one hand still wrapped around his mike,

Robbins then leaned down to the man's ear and began to speak softly to him.

You couldn't hear a word he was saying, but on the big screens you could see the man nodding ever so slightly every few seconds.

For what seemed like a full minute, Robbins continued speaking quietly into the man's ear. At one point, he picked up his hand from the man's shoulder and placed it gently on one side of his head, the way a father would with a son he was proud of. When Robbins finished, he took the man's head in his hands, looked into his eyes, and said, "Okay?"

With one small tear falling down his cheek, the man nodded.

The man's entire outlook had changed an hour later when Robbins asked him to come onto the stage and counseled him through his emotions, pausing throughout the interaction to drive home the lessons for the audience. It was a major victory that the audience felt and celebrated in a tangible way. What is so fascinating, and telling, is that my friend's outlook had changed over that time too, along with the entire room of three thousand people.

He said that the moment he watched Robbins walk down that aisle, pull back that mike, and whisper in the man's ear words for him and no one else, he knew this wasn't a typical scripted speaker with a typical hype-you-up agenda. My friend wasn't going through a major challenge and certainly wasn't suicidal. In fact, he had been mostly cynical about the whole event going into that day. He was attending on someone else's dime and was fully prepared to be disappointed by what he expected would be the same old motivational shtick.

He'd participated in the intermittent jumping and dancing to that point but only halfheartedly, feeling embarrassed and praying it would end so he could sit back down. But after that unscripted moment between Robbins and the suicidal man, my friend had no doubt that Robbins was a man he could trust. He was fully engaged the remainder of the event, which spanned four days. And in the end, he experienced a personal breakthrough of his own.

The beauty of the story is that it demonstrates the power of intuition on both ends of the spectrum—for someone who has learned to apply it effectively and for someone who is still learning that the path to success is not scripted.

If you're still leaning toward that still-learning side of the spectrum, a little wake-up call is often all it takes to remind you that the smallest measure of intuition can make a huge impact. The strength of intuition is that a little goes a long way. In other words, you don't need an equal measure of intuition and knowledge to find the right path to solution or breakthrough. You just need an ability to remain open to what you're sensing in any scenario.

I have learned to employ a modified version of the Stanislavski System from the stage. Constantin Stanislavski was a Russian-born actor and theater director who developed a method for actors to build emotional connections to their work and in turn command greater emotional responses in their audiences. In short, the method enables a performer to be both in control and reactive to any external situation by listening and adapting. Applying it requires a focus beyond the memorizing of a line and into the authenticity of the moment—being so focused on the end goal that you are able to take any number of spontaneous, responsive routes to achieve it. When you consider that there are numerous ways to convey a line in a script—in the same way that there are numerous ways to say "thank you"—this begins to make perfect sense. By listening to what the other actor is emphasizing or feeling—by truly entering into the moment—an actor can employ a more believable, more emotive line than if he simply parroted back what he had memorized from a piece of paper.

I use this same method from the stage to listen to my audience. I enter into the sixty minutes and pay attention to their "lines," which in this scenario are largely conveyed through nonverbal cues, laughs, sighs, and an overall gauge of participation. If I am attuned to these signs, and not merely the words I've planned to say or the paintings I've planned to paint, I can determine if they are a more cerebral crowd looking for additional content or a more dynamic crowd that is craving more entertainment. I can sense if my audience needs me to slow down and reinforce the gravity of my words, and I can also sense if they want me to ramp up the cadence of my rhythm and lean into the inspiration. With this intuition, I can adjust at any moment and ensure that my message continues to be well received no matter who is sitting in front of me. This can obviously be applied off the stage as well. And frankly, that is where it is more frequently needed—in your everyday conversations and interactions that probably outnumber your "stage" moments fifty to one.

The ability to remain attuned to what your customer, or your coworker, or your child, is really saying is priceless. And in truth it is the only effective, authentic way you can quickly alter the style and substance of your response to achieve superior outcomes. The magic is in your ability to hold a preconceived agenda loosely enough to remain open to the best path to success. Because the best knowledge might not be the stuff you know. And the best path might not be the one you planned.

The message is not to stop planning or cease acquiring knowledge. The message is to continue planning and learning without devaluing what you did not plan and do not know.

What is interesting about my friend's experience at the Robbins event is that he digested decades of scientific knowledge over the course of his four days: behavioral psychology, physiology, and sociology from years of studies and research. He said it was fascinating information that was presented in practical ways. And yet what made the biggest impact on him were the moments when Robbins stepped outside the science and the script—when the speaker followed his intuition.

In truth, those were not moments of intuition alone but moments when years of experience and knowledge were brought to life with gut instinct. This is the place where magic happens, or, as Cuban author Glenn Llopis puts it, where you "earn serendipity."

In his book *Earning Serendipity: 4 Skills for Creating and Sustaining Good Fortune in Your Work,* Llopis explains that what we call lucky breaks are nothing more than moments when earned experience meets practiced intuition. He cites the ability to see opportunities beyond the obvious places as the first necessary skill for earning serendipity. He calls this skill "circular vision." He explains its important effect:

You've heard it said that there is more than meets the eye, and most accept this notion blindly and without cause for action. In truth, there is always more than meets the eye. Every circumstance, every conversation, every relationship contains the potential for numerous observations beyond the obvious, and consequently, for numerous opportunities. That which meets your eye determines the opportunities available to you. And more than any other factor, the opportunities you see determine your potential for success.

Those able to see more than the obvious possess a skill that will both protect them from misfortune and point them toward good fortune.[1]

ON BEING INTUITIVE

Intuition and intellect are not in opposition to each other. In fact, they must work together if you are to reach your creative potential. While both can work independent of each other, both are more potent when paired. "Intuition becomes increasingly valuable in the new information society," wrote bestselling author John Naisbitt in *Megatrends,* "precisely because there is so much data."[2] He wrote that thirty years ago. Consider how much more true it is with the amount of knowledge we have today.

Intellect without intuition is a smart person without impact. Intuition without intellect is a spontaneous person without progress.

School and work life taught you how to grow your knowledge and sharpen your ability to put two and two together. Here's how to ensure that intuition remains in the mix of your decisions so that when two and two must equal more than four, the new solution is accessible.

1. Know What's Under the Surface

Like a compass, intuition can point us due north and let us know when we've strayed off course. It can tell us when a person isn't all he says he is. It can tell us when an opportunity is more than it might seem. It can also tell us when a solution isn't up to snuff and more investigation is required. But intuition doesn't always explain why or tell us precisely how to proceed. We want the script, and intuition isn't into scripts. It's into feelings and senses. This isn't as unstable as it sounds.

For intuition to be useful to us, we have to understand that over time and through experience we learn more than we think we do. Over time we gain verified knowledge—things we know we know—but we also gain what author Malcolm Gladwell calls a "body of submerged knowledge"—things we don't know we know. This submerged knowledge comes out in the form of intuition, and it is the one thing that according to Gladwell distinguishes experts from nonexperts:

"Anyone juggling many different variables . . . has to, at some point, rely on this body of submerged knowledge to make sense of their tasks. . . . Accurate gut feelings are things that we earn through study, experience, learning from our mistakes and steadily accumulating the kind of experiences that lead to real expertise."[3]

That means you have a body of submerged knowledge that can offer you insight for the challenges before you. The caution is that you need to know the basis of that knowledge so you don't reach beyond the effectiveness of your intuition.

If you've spent the last fifteen years in the finance industry, don't expect to have a good gut instinct for the challenges that are specific to the farming industry. Spend a season or two observing every aspect of the industry. Build your stock of verified knowledge, and as you do, your beneath-the-surface instincts will naturally swell.

This doesn't mean you can't still rely on instinct when you accept a new position or are faced with a challenge you've never seen before. In the workplace there are variables common to every situation. For example, the dynamics of relationships remain wherever you go. If you've done relationships well to this point, you already have a stockpile of relational insight above and beneath the surface. On the other hand, if you haven't been doing relationships well—maybe you're very shy or you've been accused of being overbearing—you may not have a big underground reserve. You might first need to improve your surface interpersonal skills with help from an expert before going with your gut in interpersonal situations.

Not sure what's under the surface? The only way to know is to test your intuition. Start by testing it in harmless situations that won't affect your value to your company. Friendships often serve you well in this regard. Over the course of a week, see how well you can read what people you know will do or say, or how certain situations will turn out. You're probably pretty good at this already, especially if you have a few friends you've known a long time.

This sort of testing can also be accomplished at work without major consequences. The method? When faced with problems that require a solution or circumstances that require creativity, write down your gut instincts somewhere and date them. Do this for situations that will not have a long proving season so that you can test your instincts against the actual outcomes. If you're dead on more than half the time, you have good intuition where that particular variable is concerned. Now offer it up tangibly so you can make a difference.

2. Loosen Your Processes

"Intuition," explained the distinguished medical researcher Jonas Salk, "will tell the thinking mind where to look next." Keep in mind this is Jonas Salk, the man who changed the course of history and saved millions of lives with the discovery of the polio vaccine. He was a quintessential scientist, spending hours upon hours in labs running precisely measured tests. But he was quick to confess that intuition was part of his scientific process. "It is always with excitement that I wake up in the morning," he explained, "wondering what my intuition will toss up to me, like gifts from the sea. I work with it and rely on it. It's my partner."

He understood—as did nearly every great scientist in history—that knowledge alone does not lead to the biggest breakthroughs. In fact, the more learned you become, the more dependent you should be on instinct to help you reach new heights.

Even seasoned veterans of thirty years come face to face

with problems that don't have obvious solutions and needs that require them to innovate outside their comfort zones. This is when faith in a proven process is useless.

While there will always be situations where an analysis of the data will guide you well, there will be just as many complex scenarios that require a loosening of the message the data send. Consider the process of drafting elite college football players into the NFL.

Every year when an NFL team is determining the players in whom they will invest millions of dollars, they compile hard data on each player that show precisely how big, how fast, and how strong he is. These statistics are used by team executives to create an initial profile on a player that is compared to other players at his position, currently and historically. Still, this does not guarantee a player will be a success at the professional level.

What NFL execs cannot predict with certainty is:

- How a player will respond to the increased speed and strength of the competition at the professional level
- How a player will respond to earning more money in a year than most will make in a lifetime
- How a player will interact with his teammates
- How a player will act off the field, between games and during the offseason
- How a player will respond to injury

As a result, executives also conduct one-on-one interviews and spend time with a player's family, college coaches, teammates, and friends in an effort to discover issues like a lazy streak, a prima donna mind-set, or underlying character faults. Despite their hard data, they know the stats cannot predict with certainty how well a college player will fare in the NFL. Often they must loosen their processes and go with their gut on a player who didn't have the fastest forty-yard dash but did show a high degree of character and resolve.

When it comes to your job, be prepared with all the data you can muster, but then make distinctions between the effect of knowable variables and unknowable variables. In times when simple analysis of knowable variables is enough, use it and move forward. In times when analysis cannot light the way clearly, don't lose your mind searching for more sophisticated data. Loosen your problem-solving process and let your best judgment guide you. Don't require a rationale to do so; intuition rarely has a perfect explanation. Take a leap of faith in your instincts from time to time. You won't get it right every time, but the longer you've held your job and the more often you exercise your intuition, the more accurate your gut decisions will become.

3. Make Discovery as Valuable as Data

"It is through science that we prove, but through intuition that we discover," explained the famed French mathematician Henri Poincaré. The problem is that we devote most of our attention to proving the value of what we have already done, or doing what has already been proven. The acceleration of work in the Digital Age has taught us to want quick answers to everything. If we can make a decision, create a new product, or solve a problem without having to worry ourselves with new variables, we do it. Never mind whether it's best, so long as it's not terrible. Serviceable progress, we tell ourselves, is better than slowing the pace. Breakthroughs will eventually happen.

This is the mind-set we take into most of our days. It's difficult not to with so much at stake so often. But if you don't slow down enough to put discovery back into your days, one of two things will happen: (1) you will burn out and shut down, or (2) your work will become obsolete and you will become expendable. We are not made to be data-driven machines. We need space for our personalities and individual strengths to breathe.

Discovery not only keeps your work creative and makes you more valuable to your workplace, it keeps your workplace an adventure. There is an element of mystery that arises when discovery is just as important as data. And the best jobs, says Gladwell, "are inherently mysterious."[4] They stretch us and cause us to grow, often in pleasantly surprising ways. And when employees are constantly growing, guess what is happening to the company? That's right. It's growing too—with new discoveries leading the way.

The point to remember about discovery is that it serves as a practice field for breakthrough creativity. While not every discovery will lead to a breakthrough, every discovery will build your muscles of innovation and increase your confidence in intuition. These resources will prepare you for when a major discovery is really needed.

How do you personally keep discovery as important as data in your day-to-day life? Three simple ways:

1. Remain self-critical. Our tendency is to get comfortable with our abilities on the job and turn off the self-accountability. Don't fall for it. Whether you are five years into your career or forty, your willingness to constantly critique your beliefs and test your preconceived ideas against the latest data is tantamount to your progress.

2. Submit to regular outside critique. You probably already have a regular review from your boss, but the problem with those sorts of reviews is that they typically measure progress only by data—past against present. What you need is someone who will measure your progress on the whole by asking questions like: What have you learned about yourself since last time? Have you acquired any new skills? In what ways have you increased your value to the company?

3. Listen while you work. Lift your nose from the grindstone long enough to hear what your coworkers are saying. What are they complaining about? What do they wish was better? What do they think is a waste of time/energy/resources? What are their good ideas? Remember that discovery is most effective when it's a shared endeavor. Regularly map your findings on top of others' ideas in your workplace, and foster a groundswell of potential innovation that can explode into breakthrough much quicker and more confidently than if you were starting from scratch when each challenge arose.

4. Let Conversations Be Your
Proving Ground

All of us tend toward stereotyping for various reasons, many of them not unreasonable. But our tendency to draw conclusions that are entirely determined by previous experience not only gets us in relational trouble but also keeps us from tapping our best resource for innovation and breakthrough—other people. While an apple could still fall from a tree and incite a groundbreaking idea while you are sitting solo, most of our inspirations for solutions and creativity come from interactions with others.

Consider the moment *Money* magazine called "the most profitable" of Steve Jobs's career. While Jobs was on a long car ride from Cupertino to San Francisco, his coworker Alan Kay told him about an obscure group of programmers in the computer division of Lucasfilm who created 3D graphics for medical imaging and satellite photo analysis. Kay explained that the small team's real dream was to create a computer-animated feature film using the same 3D graphics. Jobs could have cordially listened and then transitioned the conversation to matters on his agenda. (It's what many of us would do, especially if we were incredibly busy people like Jobs.) Instead he trusted his gut and asked to meet the group. Kay introduced Jobs to them shortly thereafter.

When Jobs spent time with them and observed the images they were creating, he was blown away. They were far more advanced than anything coming out of Hollywood at the time. Jobs knew nothing about the film industry—he was a fellow computer guy—but his intuition told him there was an opportunity before him he could not let pass. With his knowledge of advanced programming and a gut sense of what people would enjoy seeing on the big screen, Jobs bought the 3D graphics division of Lucasfilm and funded the programmers' dream with a $10 million investment. He also named the new company: Pixar. *Toy Story* was the programmers' dream fulfilled, but it didn't stop there. Pixar's success continued climbing until Jobs eventually sold the company to Disney for $7.4 billion.

The story is a simple illustration that makes a significant point. When you create a habit of looking beyond the obvious information in common conversations, you access a larger stockpile of opportunities that you would have otherwise never considered. From this stockpile, intuition can work its magic in concert with your current knowledge. This doesn't mean every conversation holds the keys to big success. But it does mean that more opportunities are hidden in everyday discussions than you realize.

REMAINING OPEN TO INTUITION

By the turn of the twentieth century, the urban population in America had finally surpassed the rural population. This brought with it some challenges you might expect. Challenges of architecture. Challenges of education. Challenges of transportation. One of the biggest concerns was how to deal with the increasing numbers of immigrants overlapping in urban centers. They represented many different cultures and many different ways of life. Among the most challenged groups were the children of the immigrants, who were trying not only to adjust to life itself but to adjust to the social rules of a new culture.

Thousands of these immigrant children lived in "settlement houses" run mostly by middle-class women whose service to them established the foundation of modern social work. One such worker was a woman named Neva Boyd, who served at Hull House in Chicago. Boyd was tasked with addressing the same challenge as her counterparts at other settlement houses: help the immigrant children learn English and then integrate into the multifaceted American culture around them. Many of the children were silent out of both fear and frustration with their inability to communicate their thoughts and feelings. To meet the challenge, Boyd invented games in which she embedded social lessons and the development of both intellectual and intuitive skills necessary for the children to thrive. The children were captivated by the games, and in no time they began to come out of their shells. They also began to thrive with an increasing sense of confidence in their abilities to read their surroundings and respond accordingly—in both the scripted, mannerly ways they'd been taught and spontaneous ways that allowed their wit, will, and distinct personalities to shine through.

Soon Boyd's games were adopted by the other settlement houses and then military hospitals and convalescent homes around the country as well. Boyd's legacy did not stop there. One of her assistants at Hull House was a young woman named Viola Spolin, who would take her experience working under Boyd and apply it as the head of training for a drama troupe in Chicago. Using Boyd's games as inspiration,

Spolin created what she called "theater games," which were essentially unscripted role-playing scenarios that prompted aspiring actors to open their minds and branch outside their comfort zones. Just like Boyd's immigrant children, the actors rapidly improved as they simultaneously developed the hard skills of great acting and the soft skills of intuition and its sister, improvisation.

Years later, Spolin's son Paul Sills founded the Second City, an acting troupe based solely on improvisational theater. It has become one of the most influential forces in the entertainment industry, birthing legendary shows like *Saturday Night Live, Cheers,* and *The Office* and films like *The Breakfast Club* and *My Big Fat Greek Wedding.*[5]

The important detail in that story is the common bond that unites the two groups of people mentioned: immigrants and improv actors both possess an ability to use intuition effectively, and it is what makes them so effective. We can learn from them what it means to remain open to intuition at all times.

Immigrants are not confined by the cultural patterns and expectations that funnel most of us toward predictable reactions, decisions, and outcomes. This allows them to see each opportunity objectively, as an outsider, so to speak. We've all heard of the seemingly magic advantage outsiders bring to a conversation or meeting. They have what we call "fresh eyes" that allow them to see obvious solutions and creative options that those deeply embedded in the situation can't. It is no coincidence that immigrants have co-founded more than half of the country's technology companies in the last decade.

They see and seize opportunities and solutions others simply can't.

Improv actors willingly surrender the safety of knowledge by purposefully stepping into scenarios that force them to think on the fly. Their creative genius lies in the constant exercise of their instinctive muscles. They literally use intuition every day in practice and on the stage. It is no surprise that actors whose initial training was in the art of improv are responsible for not only the shows mentioned previously but also smash hits like *M*A*S*H, The Simpsons, Mad Men, Curb Your Enthusiasm,* and *The Tonight Show.* Creativity flows from them.

What can we learn from immigrants and improv actors? This: fill your mind with information, but move forward with an objective mind-set that allows you to trust what the facts say *and* what your senses are telling you. Creative genius lies in the ability to juggle both facts and feelings until the right path is found.

Ultimately, your intuitions are the best integrators of your knowledge, experience, motives, and respect for mystery into a responsive whole. When you learn to listen to them, the irony is that you come to know more. This is why the renowned physicist Richard Feynman wrote, "A great deal more is known than has been proved."[6]

Strategize. Sense. Create.

5

be convicted

The universe is full of magical things patiently waiting for our wits to grow sharper.

—EDEN PHILLPOTTS

By industry standards, Pastor Dave Gibbons had arrived. According to Michelle Woo in a 2011 article for *OC Weekly,* by 2005 the small idea-of-a-church he'd started with seven people in his living room was now one of the fastest-growing churches in the country. Based in Orange County, California, Newsong was on its way to becoming the next Southern California megachurch. Then something changed.[1]

Gibbons was standing backstage waiting to deliver his message as the 2005 Easter service kicked off with a bang. The multiplatform extravaganza exploded in laser lights and electric guitars as a male singer belted out Creed's "What If?" while haunting phrases like "What if there was no hope?" rolled across the giant screens skirting the stage. The mostly young crowd that filled the Anaheim Convention Center was transfixed. But as Gibbons looked out over the spectacle of it all, a surprising emotion arose inside him: disillusionment.

Suddenly he found himself questioning everything he'd spent ten years building. He began asking himself questions like: *Is this what church is all about—consumer-oriented entertainment? Is this really what I set out to do?*

The parameters of success had been largely defined in his industry, particularly in California, an area of the country that spawned the megachurch movement with Calvary Chapel in Costa Mesa and the Crystal Cathedral in Garden Grove. The subsequent path for a success-minded pastor to take was well marked. Its signposts were easy to spot: multiple services, seven-figure budgets, and rock star productions on Sunday. In his early forties, Gibbons had already achieved all three with Newsong, and the church was still growing. He was a bona fide success. He'd followed the script perfectly, and now the only question was: How much more successful could he be?

Yet as he looked out over the flickering sea of faces, rock beats overwhelming his senses, that wasn't the question on his mind. He should have been on a high, yet he found himself beginning to fall into a funk. Instead of dreaming about the future, Gibbons couldn't get past how he'd arrived at a place that was so foreign to his convictions.

At the beginning, he'd believed church was about serving individuals wherever they were in life. He still believed that. But now he was about to take center stage as the leader of a church whose focus was on entertaining people en masse.

There was no individual attention in that. Something had to give.

What had happened? Where had he lost his way?

FINDING YOUR PATH

Disenchantment is a danger we all face. In the corporate world, the path to success is typically laid out before us via the history of our position—what the best before us have done—and the preestablished system into which our jobs inevitably fall—what our company is already doing to succeed. The temptation is to fall in stride without considering the options we have about what our job could or should be.

Shutting down our curiosity not only kills our creativity and makes us less potent employees, it leads to either success that doesn't satisfy or failure that is doubly disillusioning in that we've failed our responsibilities *and* our desires. Ultimately, many of us become people who work every day at a job that is neither personally invigorating nor professionally compelling. We become yes-men and -women who repress career and company growth.

In this regard, Dave Gibbons's story is a cautionary tale of what can happen when we follow a path that is detached from our desires. Even when we are successful, we are not happy. The arresting studies we read every year about dissatisfaction on the job would say this is not an uncommon mistake. One of the latest studies was initiated by the Dale Carnegie Training Institute and carried out by MSW Research in May 2012.

According to an article by Jeremy Quittner in *Inc.* magazine, from the interviews of 1,500 employees nationwide, the study reported that fewer than one-third of employees describe themselves as fully engaged with their work.[2] That's not only sad on a personal level. It's a death wish for entrepreneurs and executives trying to build vibrant companies.

But don't lose hope. These findings don't mean your fate is sealed. They are a report of where most workers are now, but they say nothing about where they can go. Your future changes when you find a way to bring your convictions to work—because your passions represent your greatest catalyst for bigger ideas and deeper engagement.

Dave Gibbons's story is not only a cautionary tale. It also illustrates what can happen when convictions begin to shape not only why you work but how you carry out your job.

The week after the Easter extravaganza, Gibbons quietly faced the revolution escalating inside him. His heart was no longer in his job. A few weeks of soul searching and prayer eventually led him to share his feelings with his staff. The announcement was a shock to the whole system he'd created. There was, however, an original investor in the audience who sensed this wasn't mere burnout or some form of midlife crisis. She told Gibbons about an opportunity to start a church in Thailand. Gibbons saw it as a chance to get away and unpack his feelings. It was there in Thailand, where the Western church protocol didn't jibe with culture, that he came to understand the problem.

The script for success he'd been following wasn't his script; it was the script his industry had defined two decades earlier, which he and his colleagues had only reinforced. Where was the creativity in that? Where was there room for churches to help meet the specific needs within their distinct locations?

Sure, good things were happening at Newsong. Some people were being inspired to some degree, and there was no reason to write the progress off as though it had been meaningless or empty. But he also couldn't continue pretending that the one-size-fits-all approach to church was what got him out of bed in the morning.

Every industry has its standard of success, whether that's an individual superstar or a flagship company. In Gibbons's case, the church industry offered a clear-cut standard that was tremendously tempting. It's hard to argue with greater popularity and bigger budgets. Yet while the pull was to follow the obvious signs, Gibbons realized they led to a definition of success that didn't move him: grow your church by attracting people like you. That wasn't his conviction of what church should be because it required choosing cultural relevance over individual needs. He explains that in the following strategy: "You're creating a one-size-fits-all piece of clothing. Then these really brilliant people, like the Mandelas or the John Lennons or the Mother Teresas, are gonna . . . reject church because it's too cookie-cutter, too processed. . . . But if you nurture them, they'll actually be the movers of the masses."[3]

In 2005, this idea flew in the face of the church industry's shining standard. While his inclination was to run from ministry altogether and start over in another industry, when Gibbons returned from Thailand he remained at Newsong but with a conviction to promote a small-picture approach to ministry. He stood before the church and shared his vision—less focus on the weekend production in favor of a main focus on getting outside the building during the week and caring for the needs of individuals in the community. In the weeks that followed, 30 percent of the members left the church. They wanted what they were used to. Gibbons pressed on without pause. He was finally following his heart. The results now speak for themselves. Newsong is no longer an up-and-coming megachurch at one giant location with a one-size-fits-all approach. It is a global village of eclectic sites from Mexico City to London to India focused on loving local individuals in tangible ways.

Today, Gibbons spends his time traveling to the different locations to offer support and leadership to the churches and communities in each place, speaking on Sundays only now and then, and primarily running a new organization he founded called Xealots (pronounced "zealots") that handpicks extraordinary people around the world and equips them to do what he did—rediscover their convictions and align them with their work in a feasible way that benefits not only themselves but those around them. While Gibbons still plays the pastoral role he has from the beginning, his rediscovered convictions have changed that role into something that is not only more beneficial to him but also more beneficial to every individual he pastors around the world. Instead of being a pastor who moves with the masses, he is now a pastor who moves the masses one person at a time.

The message is one of hope no matter how disenchanted you find yourself today or how far you feel you've already gone down someone else's path. What Gibbons couldn't gain by chasing his industry's benchmark, he achieved by following his convictions and altering his role. The personal benefit is a level of daily joy and satisfaction that his previous path couldn't produce. The professional benefit is that he has become a far more potent force through his work.

The same benefits can be yours if you're willing to rediscover and then follow your convictions. And you don't have to travel overseas or even to a new job to get things started. You can begin now, today, at the desk where you're sitting and for the company you're currently representing.

I'll explain.

FOLLOWING YOUR CONVICTIONS

There's something compelling about a person with conviction, whether or not you agree with everything he or she represents. The reason there aren't more people like this is that the prevailing pull of our existence is toward normalization. Your logical tendency is to seek out the rules, standards, and norms in any situation and conform to them. Not only is it a protective mechanism to keep you from harm, rejection, or embarrassment; it's a productive mechanism that allows you to learn language, recall lessons, and become more efficient within an existing system. But without the insight of your theoretical right brain, your dependency on norms can stunt your individual effectiveness. You become, at best, an exemplary component of the system, capable of producing only what the system is built to produce. This is why apples don't far fall from the tree and Harvard grads don't act much different from Yale grads. Systems are meant to produce predictable results. They're safe. They're sane. They provide a solid foundation. But if left unchecked they also diminish individual potency and prevent leaps forward.

The worst part is that most of us aren't aware this is happening until it has already happened, until boredom starts bubbling to the surface and disenchantment starts us wondering what's missing. Worse still, after years of yielding to norms it's common to lose sight of who we truly are. My own experience is a case in point.

After nearly a decade in the public relations business—ironically, after spending all my time knowing and promoting the unique traits of other professionals—I looked like every other suit in my industry. I had no semblance of the artist I was or what made me distinctive.

Inside me was this eclectic, innovative individual that had been all but suffocated. But once my homogenous identity had been stripped away, who I was became clear pretty quickly. I had a choice: embrace my quirks and convictions and follow where they led, or return to being the Erik Wahl an industry had molded. I chose option 1, and while it wasn't initially a cakewalk, from day one I started feeling more and more alive, even as I scribbled on pads of paper and restaurant napkins about what this new me—the real Erik Wahl—was going to mean for my career. This reinvigoration will happen in you too. But you have to first get clear on your convictions. You're going to need to get gut-honest.

Because this is a "business book" and bosses and business owners are reading it alongside employees, I'm not supposed to suggest you quit your job or find work in a foreign country for a year. But you may need to. If your work stands in stunning opposition to your convictions, you have few other options than to step away and figure out (1) where you went wrong and (2) what you need to do instead.

If that's your situation, don't hesitate. The sooner you start working with conviction, the sooner you will recapture your sense of wonder, satisfaction, and creativity on the job.

If that's not your predicament, if you're not hating work but not loving it either, you can begin recapturing your personal potency without leaving your job or living in Thailand. Start by asking yourself what you could be "convicted of" today. From there, the gaps between who you are and who you can still be will become clear. Here's what I mean:

Imagine two FBI agents showing up at your door tonight with an arrest warrant and hauling you off to jail. Within a week you find yourself sitting in a courtroom before a judge and jury with your defense attorney by your side and the prosecuting attorney at the next table over. Then suddenly, the judge asks you to stand. He begins reading from a sheet of paper the list of daily crimes for which you are being tried.

Based on your typical behavior, what would those daily crimes be? When you are eventually placed on the stand, what could you be convicted of? What in your workday are you unfailingly guilty of? We're not talking about what you do illegally. I hope for your sake nothing. We're talking about what you do consistently, habitually, passionately, so much so that there would be indisputable evidence to a jury that you are guilty of those activities—that you could actually be pegged with a descriptive title based on those activities: giver . . . taker . . . hard worker . . . slacker . . . innovator . . . excuse maker.

This isn't a trick question. I'm asking you what activities stand out in your workday so much and so often that you could be convicted of them in a court of law.

What behaviors would give the prosecution ample evidence to prove that a related trait was, in fact, who you are?

We tend to fancy ourselves something we are not—it's a great coping mechanism for our dissatisfaction, but it doesn't help us recapture who we can truly be. Often our actions don't line up with who we'd like to be or even who we think we are. If a jury of your peers had to judge who you are today, what traits would be the top three on their list?

Is there anything you do with conviction? Remember, we aren't convicted for what we think. We are convicted for what we say and do.

Now ask yourself the toughest question of all: Do the things I predominantly say and do represent my actual convictions? Does the me I bring to work represent the me I am inside?

WHAT ARE YOU KNOWN FOR?

You've probably heard the famous quote from Aristotle, "We are what we repeatedly do. Excellence, then, is not an act but a habit." It's a quote we use to define what it takes to be excellent. We focus on the second sentence and conclude that excellence takes the right habits: doing the right things at the right times over the long haul. Our left brains hear that second sentence louder because it's a line about systems.

What I've never heard the quote used for is in reference to our identity. The first line offers us that insight. If we are what we repeatedly do, then we are what we have primarily been doing. Our identity to this point is constructed by what we have repeatedly done, whether or not we might call that excellent. And that conclusion holds a truth that is desperately needed in today's world.

There was a time before the Digital Age when you earned a reputation over the course of months and years. You were known by others not by the last picture you uploaded or tweet you posted but by the consistent things you did and said during real interactions with others over the course of weeks, months, and years. Today, despite all the good that social media can do, the trap of social media is that it convinces us we can create and project an identity without actually being that person in our day-to-day life. We don't, in other words, have to live with conviction to be perceived as a person with conviction.

Consider all the causes that people—famous and not famous—attach themselves to in order to convey something about them. The truth is that the vast majority of these people have never tangibly participated in the cause with which they identify themselves. They've never been to Africa or the Middle East or their own inner city. Many are simply wearing the masks of others' convictions and completely ignoring their own.

How do you know if you are a poseur or a person of conviction?

First, consider the size of the gaps between what you'd be

convicted of by a jury of your peers and what actually moves you inside. Do people say you have a selfish tendency while you claim that serving others is a top conviction?

Second, observe what a person with conviction looks like. By your most objective conclusion, are you anything like that person?

In 1998, journalist Tom Brokaw used the phrase "the greatest generation" to describe those Americans who grew up during the Great Depression and went on to fight in World War II. These rare men and women, Brokaw argued, didn't fight for fame and fortune; they fought because it was the right thing to do. In other words, they lived lives of conviction—an entire generation of them. Perhaps you know one in your own family. One such individual was a man you've probably never heard of. His name was Walter Beran.

In 1926, he was born the fourth of four boys to German immigrants living in a small town in central Texas. There he grew up in abject poverty, picking cotton for pennies alongside his brothers, and, after eighteen months of age, without a father. And yet, had you met him at any point during that time, you would have found him to be a hardworking boy who was grateful for what he had, not what he lacked.

At seventeen, Beran enlisted in the army and soon joined his comrades in the war on the European front. Less than a year later, he was sleeping aboard the USS *Leopoldville* as it was torpedoed by a German U-boat on Christmas Eve, 1944. More than eight hundred fellow soldiers died that night, but miraculously he was not one of them. He was found floating unconscious and face up in the icy English Channel by a French tugboat captain who had seen the wreckage from the harbor and had hurried out with his men to help. Beran awoke on Christmas morning in a French hospital, where he remained for five days.

The war would end for Beran and the remaining Allied soldiers in Europe just a few months later, and he returned to Texas, where he attended college and soon met his wife, Annette. From there, Walter Beran went on to become an accountant with a firm that was then called Ernst & Ernst, today Ernst & Young. With his untiring work ethic and un-dying gratitude for every opportunity, he worked his way to the top and eventually retired in 1986 as the vice chairman of the accounting giant's western headquarters in Los Angeles.

Beran passed away in 2007, but to this day he is remem-bered as one of the most critical components of Ernst & Young's growth to one of the "Big Four" accounting firms and, according to *Forbes,* the eighth-largest private company in the United States. However, Beran's friends and colleagues would describe him more distinctly.

They would remind you that he was a man of rare convic-tion whose high character and desire for excellence drove him to take responsibility for initiating and bridging ties between Japanese and American businesses. Imagine that, from an American soldier whose friends were killed by Japanese sol-diers in the war. He was a close friend and confidant of Presi-dent Reagan on such matters, and when President Bush Sr. traveled to Japan with ARCO CEO Lod Cook, it was Wal-ter Beran they asked to join them and set up the key meet-ings. When the emperor of Japan and his wife traveled to the States in June 1994—long after Beran was retired—it was he who was asked by the White House to compile the list of invitees to a dinner in Los Angeles to honor them. And when Toyota rolled out their Lexus line for the American market, guess who received the first set of keys? Walter Beran. His friends would remind you of all that he did that reached well beyond his position with Ernst & Young.

And there is one other thing his closest friends—and especially his wife Annette—would remind you of that defined Walter Beran. The letters.

In 1964, at thirty-eight years old, Beran made a decision to write his wife a letter every night he was away from their home on business. His workload had increased steadily since his first year on the job, and now his time on the road was ramping up. It was clear that to continue excelling in his position he would need to visit clients and prospects around the country every month. Hard work was a conviction he held, as was the Golden Rule. He also held a conviction to love Annette as best as he knew how and make sure she knew there was no more important person in his life. The letters would make sure of this.

In September 1964, Beran penned his first letter to his wife from a hotel four hours down the road from their home in San Antonio. Two weeks before he retired on September 30, 1986, Beran penned a final letter to her from the road. The letters—nearly 1,300 of them or approximately five every month of his career—were a conviction he lived out for twenty-two years.

Beran's left brain told him to put his nose to the grindstone and get things done. "Be industrious," it told him. But his right brain reminded him that how and why he got things done was just as important. "Be aware," it said. So he was both industrious and aware. Walter Beran was one of the best employees his company ever had. But it wasn't because he followed the company's employee handbook. It was because he saw his job as a large canvas on which to paint the convictions of his heart. The result is a vibrant portrait of a life that still inspires the world today.

ON BEING CONVICTED

"Don't ask what the world needs," clarified the great civil rights leader Howard Thurman. "Ask yourself what makes you come alive and go do that. Because what the world needs is people who have come alive."[4]

One of the greatest forces in the world is the pull toward uniformity. In our longing for gratifying days where our best selves are put to work and inspired to flourish, we look outside ourselves for direction when we should be looking inside. While those who live with great conviction can always inspire you, they cannot lay out your path for you because they are not you. They do not know what you truly desire. Only you can ask: What makes me come alive? And only you can go do that in your work.

Here's how.

1. Do the Next Thing on Your Heart

Oswald Chambers was a chaplain to Australian and New Zealand soldiers stationed in Zeitoun, Egypt, during World War I. The soldiers were mostly young men with a lot ahead of them, and they had many questions about what life would bring. After a few weeks with them, Chambers sensed they were itching for something that would take their minds off the war—something that would give them hope in their future after the fighting was done. It was an understandable desire given their circumstances. They were looking for the road map out of their situation. It was what they were fighting for. How could they know what God wanted them to do with their lives? If they knew this, they surmised, it would help them get through the immediate battles before them.

Chambers was compassionate toward the men, but he was also too fatherly to sugarcoat matters. He knew they wanted to know the path to happiness and success and longevity. He also knew there was no answer he could give them that would fully satisfy their hopes. So he offered this advice: "If you want to know God's will for your life, do the next thing he asks you to do." It was his way of telling them, "If you want to know how to have the life you desire, follow your heart today."

It's brilliant advice.

We tend to trivialize today. We spend hours and days and weeks determining the precise destination we desire. And then we gloss over our daily behaviors as if they don't matter, as if we will arrive at our desired destination no matter what we do. We are, in other words, all talk much of the time.

The thing we so often miss is that the road map from where we are to where we want to arrive is traveled, step by step, by following our convictions. We often don't know where our convictions will lead us. But following them is our only guarantee of peace, satisfaction, and joy in our days. It's the small-picture mind-set we truly need in the midst of all the big-picture thinking.

Let me be candid: the big picture doesn't matter as much as you think, and the small picture matters a lot more than you realize. The big picture can be inspiring, but the small picture of one day is the only context in which the big picture will become a reality.

This is just as true with big problems as it is with big dreams. Big problems don't get big from one big action. They get big from small actions compounded over time. To solve big problems, you have to solve your small actions. To follow big dreams, start by following small, daily convictions.

For example, in the many interactions you will have over the course of the next week, ask yourself, "Who must I be?" not "Who am I expected to be?"

2. Be a Catalyst

There is nearly always a way to work with conviction without putting off everyone around you. Following your convictions is not about being isolated. It's about taking heartfelt action within the context of collaboration. Conviction without collaboration is called "tyranny." Conviction without compassion is called "dictatorship." I don't suggest you attempt either at work, or anywhere for that matter. The greatest movements occur, not because one person is forcing others to follow his personal convictions, but because others share similar convictions and find courage to act on them when one person stands up first. This is the place where a good idea can swell to a groundbreaking idea, simply because someone had the conviction to be the initial spark.

The truth is that while our convictions are formed in us from various circumstances and diverse beliefs, they are ultimately not as unique as we might think. A worker who remains committed to being home for family dinner no matter what is going on at work might inspire a coworker to visit her grandmother in assisted living every Saturday morning, no matter how busy life gets. The shared conviction is one of keeping family a priority.

An executive who keeps a commitment to openly admitting mistakes will soon find dozens of workers who step up and confess mistakes—not because responsibility is one of the company's core tenets but because they share a conviction that honesty leads to quicker solutions and more sustainable progress. In this way, working with conviction acts as a catalyst not only for bringing out your best effort and brightest ideas but for bringing out the same in others.

Don't be afraid to be who you are compelled to be.

Are you passionate about something at work? Don't stuff your emotions because you fear being "too much" for others to handle.

Are you a compassionate person who is fed up with how a coworker is treating others? Step up and be a leader. Confront the coworker assertively and respectfully. Be a representation of the person you'd want others to be if you'd been wronged.

The best kind of conviction is truly contagious. It can

even turn a perceived threat into an ally. Consider an event that was a hallmark of Sheriff Bob Braudis's long career.

Braudis served as the sheriff of Pitkin County in Aspen, Colorado, for twenty-four years. In his book *The Seven Arts of Change,* author David Shaner tells about when he worked as a deputy under Sheriff Braudis, a large, six-foot-four man who fit the stereotype of a hard-nosed cop. Though he looked tough, as soon as you met him you quickly learned that he was a compassionate man who held a deep conviction to protect the people of Aspen through nonviolent means—even from themselves.

One case in point occurred when Sheriff Braudis was the patrol director one evening and a call came through dispatch that a gunman was holding the patrons of a local tavern hostage. Braudis was the first to arrive on the scene and quickly assessed the situation, then approached the door with his hands visible and no gun drawn. From the door he talked to the man and attempted to understand his pain. Braudis learned he had recently separated from his wife and she was keeping him from seeing his daughter. When he saw his daughter in the restaurant, the man's own convictions got the best of him and he pulled out a gun so that no one could keep him from her.

Sheriff Braudis saw that the man was just manifesting his love for his daughter in a harmful way and that it was truly not directed at anyone in the tavern. Sensing the sheriff's compassion, the man eventually let Braudis in the door. There Braudis continued to talk to the man about the consequences of his actions, namely, that he would probably be guaranteed to not see his daughter again if he didn't turn himself in.

"His empathy toward the man's rage validated the suspect . . . ," explains Shaner. "In short, Bob put himself in the man's shoes, and the more the man talked with Bob, the more he realized that much of his anger was with himself. He eventually put down his weapon. The man's whole demeanor then changed."[5]

It's a great story because it shows the difference between right and wrong expressions of conviction. One man held a conviction any parent shares—he loved his child more than life itself. But he let his conviction make him forget those around him. This is where conviction is perilous.

Sheriff Braudis, on the other hand, kept his conviction in context. No matter where his job took him, he couldn't escape the fact that what he did involved other people. He understood that for his conviction to be a positive catalyst he had to apply it in a way that would benefit others—even if they didn't see the benefit at first.

This is the true force of conviction: it unites. And if you can unite others to a cause, an idea, a solution, you are not only a regular catalyst for innovation and growth but a leader no company can do without.

Be convicted. Be a catalyst.

6

be accelerated

If the rate of change on the outside exceeds the rate of change on the inside, the end is near.

—JACK WELCH

am often asked why I don't do traditional paintings. Why do I create only paintings
that I can do in three minutes as opposed to spending
weeks or months perfecting one piece, as most painters do?

The short answer is I don't have the patience. My
mind is always racing with new ideas, and spending
months staring at the same canvas sounds, to me, on
most days, like a slow death. But that's not the whole
story.

The long answer is that I see great value in acceleration.

I paint quickly because I want to deliver my art in
real time via a live performance. I believe my work
stands a far better chance of being both seen and understood in this context. A sixty-minute live performance is a more effective way to connect with and

inspire my audience than, for instance, asking you to go to a gallery and "view" one of my paintings. There's no human connection in that. No direct way for me to make an impact on your life.

So instead of laboring in obscurity for months to produce one inert product, I aim to shake you awake by creating a painting in person in far less time than you ever thought possible. From this interaction between us, a connection is made. From this connection, progress can be made. And progress, not art, is my ultimate goal.

I am less interested in creating photorealistic art and more interested in how I can "perform" a painting by capturing image likeness in the fewest strokes possible. I want to convey that creativity is far more accessible and attainable than we realize, once we break from the systems and scripts that have governed our actions in the past. Acceleration amplifies the emotion of the moment, and it simplifies the message I want you to hear. In the end, I know the ideas that gain the most traction are the simplest ones. This is why Leonardo da Vinci said, "Simplicity is the ultimate sophistication." And simplicity is a forced necessity when you've chosen to move fast.

This sums up the choices I've made—accelerated output, simple message, immediate impact. It's the path you should take too if you want to reach a new level of creative effectiveness on the job.

I won't tell you it's easy to make these choices. Your left brain will always cry out for a controlled, calculated speed when approaching any task, especially those with high importance. It will tell you to hold the wheel with both hands . . . watch your speed . . . make no sharp or sudden turns . . . verify you have the most accurate directions . . . be certain of your destination before you begin . . . and make sure you use the bathroom first!

How would you like to take a summer-long road trip with your left brain? Sounds wonderful? Maybe if you are eighty-five. Most of us would admit that kind of trip sounds boring, if not agonizing. You'd be more inspired reading an article in a travel magazine. Unfortunately, your career probably resembles that road trip if you're always pumping the brakes at every turn.

Without some high-speed adventure, security is only a facade. And progress is uninspiring. If you are listless, you're playing it too safe. It's time you push the gas pedal.

Acceleration changes the game. And the irony is that it ultimately gives you a greater sense of peace and satisfaction than when you feel completely in control. Here's why.

PROGRESS DOES NOT REQUIRE PERFECTION

A freeing benefit of accelerating output is that perfection is not the standard. Progress is. When progress is the framework for your tasks, you are not limited by the right directions. You are not limited by what worked well in the past. You are not decelerated by overanalysis. Instead, you are free to blaze trails, to let ideas fly—the more the better. Failure is not only an option; it's a likely outcome. But in an accelerated context, you make the choice to let failure show you a better way, not slow you down. Failure is just one of the guideposts along the way. This doesn't mean you're aiming for failure. It just means you're not trying to prevent failure before you begin.

Accelerated output is responsible for the sense of adventure you had at your fingertips when you were young. Because you didn't have a database of cause-and-effect scenarios weighing you down, you rarely balked at an opportunity. As you grew older and that database increased, you increasingly weighed pros and cons before moving forward. You were learning to pump the brakes at every turn. Now, as an adult, you are a brake-pumping pro.

Most of us aim for a pace of output in which we can always make calculated decisions. There are two primary problems with this strategy:

1.   You will find it difficult to accelerate when faced with challenges or opportunities that require speed to succeed.

2.   You will never tap into your best resources or know the maximum rate at which you can progress.

There are plenty of mediocre employees who are content with predictable progress. They are on time every day. They have safe haircuts and smart wardrobes. They speak softly and follow their job description to a "t." They are dependable and consistent. They are the least likely to get canned for breaking company rules. But they are also the least likely to come up with a game-changing idea. And they are not the employees you'd want to have to depend on in crunch time. They are the ones who have the most trouble increasing their pace or adapting at a rapid clip—and these days, the need for quick change occurs often.

On the other hand, employees—and businesses as a whole—who are practiced in being nimble are far more likely to experience breakthroughs and far more able to adjust to changes of any size.

This doesn't mean you shouldn't be well versed in certain aspects of your job. It doesn't mean you shouldn't establish systems that give some strategic order to your calendar—the left brain still has a meaningful purpose. While the left brain plays an important role in making innovations a reality, the right brain is the originator of those innovations. Studies have shown that while strategy and focus play an important role in the creative process, we ultimately need a jolt to get an insight.[1]

What this means is that you have to remain as well versed at accelerating—at being jolted—as you are at maintaining a consistent pace. Since homeostasis is your comfortable default, you may need to impose acceleration on yourself in order to ignite greater creativity, prepare yourself for change, and uncover valuable resources you didn't know you had—all the while keeping progress as the goal, not perfection. Here's what I mean:

While I spend time in my studio practicing my performance of every painting, and while I continue to study art history and technique, I don't aim to trace the academic rules of great art with my finished work. I am not creating a product to be hung in a museum and praised by curators and art critics for decades to come. I am creating a product to evoke feelings that will compel you to take bolder, more innovative, more authentic actions now, today. I don't need three months or three years to create something that makes that sort of impact. I need three minutes. You may need even less time.

The standards of creativity in the real world—especially the business world—are not the same as they are at the Louvre or at Sotheby's. To be more innovative, to be a greater creative asset to your company, you do not need ideas that will be lauded by economists and MBA students for the next century. You need ideas that spark greater collaboration, better products, stronger customer loyalty, and ultimately a bigger bottom line.

Notice I said "spark" and not "produce." This is where most people go wrong with creativity. They see a finished product like an iPhone and say, "Steve Jobs is a creative genius. Look what he created!" While Jobs was obviously creative, he didn't dream up the iPhone one night, lock himself in a room with some raw materials and specialized tools, and then reappear a week later with the first iPhone in his hand. It was nothing like that. For starters, Jobs had a lot of help. Second, the iPhone didn't even begin with an idea. It began with a problem—and Jobs was simply the spark that ignited the need for a solution.

In a *Slate* magazine article, Farhad Manjoo explains that "by 2005 . . . the music player that rescued Apple from the brink now faced a looming threat: the cell phone. Everyone carried a phone, and if phone companies figured out a way to make playing music easy and fun, 'that could render the iPod unnecessary,' Steve Jobs once warned Apple's board."[2]

Fortunately, as Manjoo points out, the cell phones on the market at the time sucked. They were good for making calls and little else. Those that attempted to offer other functions were clunky and frustrating to use, primarily because the only input methods were hard keys, like those on a Black-Berry, which made it difficult to navigate, or a touchscreen that required a stylus. Finger presses could not yet be detected.

However, Jobs still sensed that a phone maker would someday solve the interface problem and create a superphone that did more than make calls—a phone that played music and videos and whatever else someone could dream up—a device that would make the iPod obsolete.

Apple's survival, according to Manjoo, depended on creating that product itself. Two years later, Jobs introduced the world to the first iPhone.

The story illustrates the collaborative nature of creativity that we often overlook. Embracing this aspect of creativity will help you employ a more whole-brained approach to your work. What companies need are not a bunch of one-stop-shop iPhone creators. In other words, you don't need to produce a Mona Lisa in order to add creative value. What companies need are people who are willing to work with a continual sense of urgency to raise the bar in any facet of their business: people who never pump the brakes on quality improvement, who never hit the cruise control because the current system is working, and who never rely on past road maps to direct future paths because they know the best road map is awareness.

Jobs's creative genius was not in crafting the masterpiece of innovation known as the iPhone. It was in igniting a creative bonfire with a simple idea on how to solve a looming problem with Apple's most lucrative product. Jobs didn't create the masterpiece; he sparked the fire from which it emerged. This is how masterpieces in business are created.

If you can begin to see creativity through this lens—accelerated output, simple message, immediate impact—you will instantly begin to see where you can invigorate your days and add more value to your company.

The simplest definition of great art is that it engages and inspires. You are capable of doing both through your work habits on any given day. You just have to get past the masterpiece misconception. This is the belief that if your offerings to your coworkers, customers, and bosses aren't perfect, you shouldn't bother offering them. You should just let your ideas marinate awhile . . . keep your mouth shut in the meantime . . . let someone else take the risk . . . be happy you get a paycheck . . . don't try to be a hero—just do your job.

It's a left-brained cop-out.

Perfection is the standard we hold up when we need an excuse to justify our fear of rejection or failure. Consider how many of us react when we are put on the spot in an important meeting. "What do you think?" we are asked. It's at that point we need a logical reason to keep hugging the tree trunk and not go out on a limb. And so we often retract into our safety shells under the pretext of not wanting to sound stupid or waste the boss's time or, God forbid, be wrong. We give the pat answer, if any answer at all.

This posture is a main reason why companies struggle with creativity. Too many people are searching for perfection. The perfect solution. The perfect product. The "Failure isn't an option" gong is banged quite often. All it does is clam everyone up. Wanting to avoid humiliation or failure, our left brains kick into protective mode. They assert, "The less you say the better," or "Don't say anything unless it's gold." It's very tempting advice. In fact, I have to fight following it every time I take the stage.

If you've seen more than one of my shows, you know there is an element of consistency to them. While I don't continually paint the same paintings or say precisely the same words, I aim to convey a similar message using similar means. That can make hitting the cruise control very tempting. It can make me not want to take any new risks on stage because I have a good thing going. I know what I'm doing. It's working. Why then would I take the stage and try to reinvent a product that works and in the process risk embarrassing myself and dinging my brand?

Progress. That's why.

I don't want to be where I am five years from now. I don't want to be here even five weeks from now. Not only do I want to continually improve as a person, I want to continually improve as a performer. Therefore, I cram as much insight and inspiration into my sixty minutes on stage as is humanly possible. I know there's still more I can do. So I keep pushing myself forward. I continue accelerating.

Are there times when I become consumed with insecurity at a critical moment and return to what is most comfortable? Absolutely. Instead of attempting the new painting I've never performed before, I default to doing a painting that comes easy. Or instead of sharing a new explanation that just came to mind, I offer an explanation that I've used at previous performances because I don't want to fumble with my words and look foolish. This isn't just a once-in-a-while occurrence either. It's quite regular. I have to fight the gravity of mediocrity nearly every time I take the stage. I push myself to break free from that pull every day. It doesn't pay off every time, but it pays off over time.

At one show I was not at all prepared to pull off a portrait of Steve Jobs upside down, but I knew I wanted to. I knew it was the right time to do it. I could have done what was most comfortable. I could have gone with a standard protocol, and I think the crowd would have been saying, "That was neat." But this was within a week's time of Jobs's death. He was on the minds of every person in that room in one way or another. I thought, "If there's any time to seize the moment and take a risk, this is it. If I fail, I fail."

That risk ended up sparking a huge success. But I've taken that risk before and failed. I beat myself up over it. But I don't stop risking. I've learned to not slow down. Over time, I've grown to love the sense of adventure that never dies when you remain accelerated.

Don't fool yourself into believing the masterpiece misconception. You don't need perfection to make progress. You just need a spark to fuel a fire of improvement. That's true of both personal growth and corporate growth. Improvement comes more quickly and steadily when you are willing to let sparks fly often—even if that means a greater rate of failure.

CREATE FOR THE TRASH CAN

Certain writers throughout history believed you could create only one great book in your lifetime. Certain painters throughout history believed a similar message about paintings. On one hand, I understand this view. If I were going to create my life masterpiece—the one product that would embody my best skills, spirit, and persona and establish my legacy for all time—I would take some time working on it, let it marinate for weeks, months, maybe even years. I wouldn't stand on a stage and paint it in three minutes.

On the other hand, I am not looking to create one masterpiece, and I don't agree that it's all we have to offer. When the sparks are flying every day, a lot can happen—a lot you could have never dreamt up in your most lucid moments. So I look to create as many sparks as possible. I accelerate to scale my impact and increase the likelihood of a breakthrough idea. Instead of spending all my time mapping out my masterpiece, I paint for the trash can.

This isn't my way of bowing out of maximum effort. And it's not my way of trying to preempt the rejection of buyers or critics who might say my art doesn't stand up to museum standards. It is my way of creating a lab in which I am not limited by flawlessness. If what I paint is for the trash can, I am free to rapidly explore, dream, and discover without the risk of failure. I treat my speaking the same way. I don't care to study speakers or attend speaking classes to learn how to talk in front of a crowd. I feel that they are using outdated models on how to "educate" an audience (opening thesis, three main points, closing summary). It's tidy and efficient, but predictable and uninspiring. Instead, I get my best ideas from live performances. I am interested in what live entertainers are doing to engage an audience. I want to know what Bono, Bruce Springsteen, and Bob Dylan do to rapidly inspire fifty thousand fans. I study the timing of Jerry Seinfeld and Bill Cosby to understand how to immediately hold an audience captive. I study DJs like Tiësto, Skrillex, and Deadmau5 to understand human biorhythms and anticipation and their relationship to toggling the emotions of an audience multiple times over the course of a single song. All are experts in accelerated output. And all have progressed further than their contemporaries.

Generally speaking, I study them because I believe art precedes business. Art is the tricked-out concept car helping us understand where we can be five years from now. It is the leading indicator for business strategy, and if we are to learn from art, not only must we study gifted artists doing their thing, but we must become artists ourselves.

One message that today's art offers every businessperson is that growing innovation and impact don't require multiple brainstorming sessions and quarterly pep rallies. They simply require an environment that pushes for accelerated output balanced with a higher tolerance for failure. There are risks, yes. But none are greater than stagnation.

ON BEING ACCELERATED

Progress requires making strides. And the quicker the stride, the greater the progress. Don't buy into the notion that you can take a giant leap if you spend enough time carefully mapping it out. By the time you get done planning, others will have lapped you twice and already taken that leap you spent months mulling over. Opt instead to "just go" and let the sparks fly. You will make mistakes. Learn quickly and keep moving. Along the way, you will refine your skills, rekindle adventure, and ignite a new level of creativity you didn't know you had.

Here are two guidelines for acceleration.

1. Refine Your Resources . . . Even When You Don't Have To

Ever notice the effect immediacy has on us? If a much-needed vacation is approaching and the last thing you want is to take work with you to that beach resort, what happens? You suddenly find a gear you didn't know you had. Your focus becomes laserlike. Your time management is flawless. Your sentences become more clear and concise. You have zero trouble saying no to less important matters. You don't overthink anything. You work with a polished combination of instinct and skill. You are suddenly the most effective employee in your position that the company has ever known.

What does that say? It definitely proves vacation is very important to you. But it also proves you can be far more effective than you are on a typical workday. What if you could call up that level of effectiveness on any given day? What if that became your operation mode?

Your typical work mode is probably not ineffective. It keeps you out of trouble and even garners you a nice pat on the back every now and then. But it's not going to ignite any breakthroughs if it's never tested.

When Steve Jobs regained control of Apple in the mid-1990s, one of his top priorities was fixing Apple's tarnished image. The company had lost its shirt since he resigned in 1985, and it needed a new vision fast. Jobs took back the wheel and hit the gas pedal. He immediately rehired Lee Clow and his team from Chiat\Day to help him come up with a plan. They presented him with a new slogan for Apple's ads: Think Different.

Once the idea was approved, Jobs gave Clow's people seventeen days to complete the entire campaign, which included a television commercial and supporting billboards. It was far too short a time frame by normal standards. But Jobs quickly pulled some strings with a few celebrity friends, and Clow and company put their resources on overdrive.

What resulted is now one of the most iconic ad campaigns of all time. It began with a black-and-white television commercial featuring numerous game changers like Einstein, Dylan, Branson, Edison, Ali, Callas, Earhart, Hitchcock, and Picasso. It first aired on September 28, 1997. I'm sure you've heard the script:

Here's to the crazy ones. The misfits. The rebels. The troublemakers. The round pegs in the square holes. The ones who see things differently. They're not fond of rules. And they have no respect for the status quo. You can quote them, disagree with them, glorify or vilify them. About the only thing you can't do is ignore them. Because they change things. They push the human race forward. And while some may see them as the crazy ones, we see genius. Because the people who are crazy enough to think they can change the world, are the ones who do.[3]

The key to igniting better creativity is often little more than a shift in mind-set. When a deadline looms and your job is on the line, the shift happens naturally. You go into hyper-resourceful mode. MacGyver survival mode. It's a different story when you're sitting in your cubicle fulfilling your typical duties with no impending doom. It's easy in that scenario to simply get things done without imagination.

How do you go into hyper-resourceful mode when the deadline isn't looming? Start by challenging yourself to win the day. Set an audacious daily goal and fight to meet it the way you would if failure meant you'd be fired. Remove all distractions and time sappers that stand in the way. Focus and call up on every resource. And determine your reward if you meet the goal. Make it something worthwhile. Dinner at your favorite restaurant. A mini–shopping spree.

The following day, go back and review the tape, so to speak. What resources rose up that surprised you? What thing did you do wrong that you could easily remedy? This is more than a game you play with yourself. You are essentially taking inventory on your creative storehouse. And the more you do it, the more refined your resources will become. The more refined they become, the more rapidly and naturally you will be able to ignite your creativity whenever it is needed.

2. Refuse to Be Overwhelmed

When facing a problem, take your attention off what's wrong. When commencing an important activity, take your attention off potential negative outcomes. Both will cause you to react emotionally and proceed with caution and pessimism. This is a surefire way to bottle up your resourcefulness, default to old solutions, and even invite disaster.

Instead, remain optimistic. And relax.

"Decades of research demonstrate that optimists get better results in all areas of life," says author Michael Gelb. " . . . Since your brain is the. most profoundly powerful solution-finding mechanism in the known universe, your chances for success are much greater when you embrace problems as opportunities for resourcefulness and creativity."[4] And according to the neuroscience blog Neural Sense, "Relaxing results in a burst of alpha waves in the brain, which have been shown to be crucial in the discovery of new ideas. These alpha waves may generally be followed by a spike of gamma waves . . . associated with the binding of neurons, or the formation of insights."[5]

But relaxing is not merely a tool to incite creativity. It's a necessary skill when you're traveling at high speed and taking in information for rapid-fire decisions. With global connectivity now the standard, this scenario seems to define the nature of business in most industries today. If you can keep from being overwhelmed, you have a distinct advantage.

In *The Seven Arts of Change,* author David Shaner offers an illustration of this advantage from his experience as a world-class downhill skier in the early 1970s. He explains that even when you factor in the slow start of the gate, in World Cup races you easily average over 60 mph. "Up to about 45 mph, you feel in control," he writes. "Above that speed, a new feeling arises." He continues:

*The race becomes more like a swift dance as you con-
stantly search for ways to bend with the mountain's
curves to maintain stability and produce more speed. . . .
Downhillers cannot out-muscle the forces of momentum
and gravity. We had to find our inner strength to keep
us physically relaxed, emotionally calm and mentally focused. This was the only way to finish the race successfully
and in one piece.*[6]

Shaner, a seasoned change consultant for Fortune 500
companies for more than thirty years now, goes on to describe a near-death experience during a World Cup downhill
race in the 1970s on a shoddily prepared course in Argentina.
The two skiers before him had crashed badly on the final section before the finish line. Unbeknownst to him, both were
lying unconscious and in pools of blood . . . and directly in his
path. Because the competitors had been sent only one minute
apart, Shaner had already left the gate before course officials
could radio the top to stop sending skiers. By the time he
reached the last section of the course, his speed had reached
90 mph.

On a normal run, at that speed, the smallest adjustment
can make the difference between first and last place. On this
day, the stakes were much higher. The pointed tips or sharp
edges of his skis could easily impale a fellow skier if he hit
them. A collision could also send him into a deadly long-
distance tumble. Fortunately, Shaner had been thoroughly
trained in what he calls "the art of relaxation."[7]

When he spotted the first immobile skier, he immediately
straightened his body to allow the counterforce of the wind to

slow his speed, and then he relaxed his lower body. It was just enough to allow his skis to glide slightly to one side of the first skier and narrowly miss the second to the other side.

"I survived," he concludes, "but the margin of survival was extremely slight. The only real difference between me and my fellow racers was a quick visual cue and an ability to relax under pressure."

Shaner's conclusion could just as easily be describing the survival of a company during a down economy, or your survival during a major push to meet a lofty quota. Acceleration often defines the landscape of our work environments with or without our permission. It makes sense then to ensure that it is an advantage and not an adversary. The ability to relax is the key because it has two critical benefits: (1) it keeps your full arsenal of resources available, and (2) it keeps you nimble enough to use them rapidly.

Simply put, relaxation is the key to allowing your resourcefulness to flow freely, and more rapidly when necessary. If you can learn to relax in an accelerated context, not only will you survive the toughest tests, but you will remain innovative even when others around you are balled up on the floor.

How do you relax when the stakes are high and the scenery is blowing by you?

First, focus on what you can control. Often the majority of our anxiety in accelerated environments has to do with elements we cannot control, like style points and the opinions of others. Don't spend needless energy on being precise or keeping everyone happy. These are unrealistic objectives in steady environments—virtual impossibilities in accelerated ones. Be messy if you must and let the safety patrol worry themselves sick, while you scrap your way to a solution.

Second, be okay with failure. Remember that creativity is making something from nothing. It will always require that you take risks. There is always the potential that you will waste time, waste money, and harm your own or your company's reputation. These risks are even higher when you're moving fast. This is more than rational minds can handle. Simply knowing that the likelihood of failure has increased scares most away. Don't let it scare you. Don't let it slow you down. Use your best judgment, be a quick study, and keep moving.

Know that the most innovative people in history—the "crazy ones," as the Apple ad called them—failed often, usually far more often than those around them. But that was not because they were less prepared or more ignorant.

Numerous studies have shown that the most highly creative people fail more simply because they try more often. They accelerate their output. As a result, they don't necessarily have better ideas; often they just have more ideas from which to choose.

To be the artist you can be, sooner and more often, accelerate your output, refine your resources, and relax. You won't always be perfect. You won't always put smiles on everyone's faces. But you will always increase the likelihood of a breakthrough.

Accelerate to innovate more.

be spontaneous

Mystery is at the heart of creativity. That, and surprise.

—Julia Cameron

've been asked how I navigate the modern reputation of graffiti as a form of property destruction. In response I always explain that graffiti hasn't always had this reputation. It was only in the last century that graffiti was hijacked by vandals and tagged with the perception of destruction. In its purest form, it began on ancient cave walls. We etched and colored our discoveries, our dreams, and our history. It was how we artfully captured and remembered our stories.

In this view, graffiti is not the destruction of property. But it can be the destruction of old paradigms—at least if I have my way. I want my work to reclaim the original identity of graffiti and remind you to etch a truer, more distinctive story on the walls of your company. But to do that, I need to shock you into seeing something about yourself that you probably can't see in a predictable work environment. Graffiti serves a purpose here too, through spontaneity.

When I take the stage for sixty minutes at a corporate event, I could simply give a compelling speech about rediscovering your creative genius and show you some great art and supporting quotes along the way. But I doubt you'd be as inspired as when I storm a stage with music cranked high and, without a word, fill a four-foot canvas with the face of a luminary in a matter of three minutes. That's the other effect of graffiti I use to my advantage. Unlike traditional painting, it is always spontaneous. And spontaneity inspires.

But the truth is that I am not aiming to be merely inspirational. I am aiming to convince you to be spontaneous yourself; to create your own graffiti. I've learned that when spontaneity is of your own doing, your creativity climbs to a new level.

THE PATH OF GREATER POSSIBILITIES

Ongoing spontaneity is critical to creativity because it forces you to see your surroundings differently, to consider possibilities you never considered before. Suddenly, your steps and destination are not scripted. For a time, your story becomes a mystery. And mystery, as the gifted author and artist Julia Cameron says, "is at the heart of creativity."

Here's why that's true.

Mystery feeds curiosity, and curiosity compels us to consider new patterns, forge new paths, ask what more is possible than we previously thought. The irony is that when we chase mystery we find, more often than not, that these new possibilities are not new at all. They were always available to us, yet hidden by our tightly framed expectations and pre-conceived notions—even our stereotypes. Our story scripts are suddenly blown aside, and we see things not as we think they are but as they truly are. We discover that we are more capable and more extraordinary than we ever imagined we were.

Every now and then we see this truth on a global stage. The explosion of reality television has its downsides, but an upside is that we get to witness moments like the one that occurred on *Korea's Got Talent* on June 6, 2011, when twenty-one-year-old Choi Sung-Bong took the stage before the judges and a full house for the first time.

Choi had been abandoned to an orphanage at three years old. At five, he ran away to escape physical abuse. He survived on the streets selling gum and energy drinks to passersby and sleeping in public restrooms. At eight, Choi began working as a delivery boy and a day laborer but was subsequently sold as a modern-day indentured servant. For the next decade, he remained homeless, passed between people he could trust and those he could not. Along the way, he met two inspired souls who saw beyond the battered exterior of the young boy. The first, a woman who ran a food cart outside a nightclub, helped him pursue an education and complete his elementary and middle school GED. The second, a music teacher, gave Choi voice lessons for free.

On June 6, 2011, the young man who stood before the crowd was still timid and spoke with a slight voice. The path he had taken didn't offer any indication of what might be. Then he began to sing, and a mystery was unveiled.

The song was "Nella Fantasia," originally sung by famed soprano Sarah Brightman in 1998. In English, the song means "In My Fantasy"—a perfect title for what ensued.

The moment Choi opened his mouth, a sense of awe overtook the judges and audience. As the song escalated, mouths fell open and eyes filled with tears. This astonishing voice . . . from an abused, homeless boy. Yes. One female judge leaned forward on her elbows in utter disbelief, her mouth open and her hands holding her temples as if to keep her skull from exploding. When the song was finished, the inhibited Choi nodded slightly as the crowd and judges burst into applause. A single, unexpected moment had rewritten the script. Suddenly, the black-and-white picture of Choi Sung-Bong had erupted in colors. A foregone conclusion became an international sensation.[1]

These same unveiling moments are before you, if you will let spontaneity lead you.

THE BRIDGE TO BEYOND

In simplest terms, spontaneity is a bridge to mystery. And mystery is what opens our eyes to new possibilities for, and from, our work.

We all love mystery, just in other people's stories. It's a different story when the mystery involves us. Suddenly the unknown is not nearly as appealing. Suddenly the unknown becomes frightful. We do not wonder what greater potential lies ahead; we wonder what peril lies ahead.

This is your left brain crying out.

It reminds you that what is safest is to stay in the world of what is known. What it doesn't tell you is that the known world is also the world of stagnation. No growth. No break-throughs. Nothing new. The law of the land is the law of diminishing returns. New becoming old. Beauty becoming bland. Life moving toward death. Allowed to lead, your left brain will keep you alive, but you'll be dying a little more every day.

To counterbalance your left brain's cries for safety, you must let your right brain lead you into spontaneous moments: saying yes even when your schedule says no . . . extending a hand even when your hands are full . . . offering the hard truth when protocol instructs you to be agreeable.

Big-picture thinking has been a buzzword for a couple of decades. It is the left brain's version of innovation. It convinces you that if you strategize enough about what can be, you can avoid taking any real chances along the way. You can avoid the need for spontaneity. Ironically, what we miss in our efforts to employ big-picture thinking is the small opportunities before us every day to act spontaneously and thereby expand our stories in far greater measure.

Simply knowing where you want to go will not get you there. It is one thing to map out your destination. It is another thing to take the steps down the path, especially when you consider that a career in business is far more like navigating the Wild West than navigating the geometric grid of a modern city. While the big picture can entice us with its grand promise, it can also fool us with its utter simplicity. Preparation for our journey requires far more than possessing a mere map.

Steve Scanlon of Building Champions is one of the most sought-after career coaches in the country.[2] He has earned this reputation not because he is a great strategist, laying out flawless career maps that ensure his clients will keep moving confidently up the rungs of the ladder. His reputation is largely the result of his ability to teach his clients what he calls "small-picture thinking." If you were sitting with him, he would remind you that the big picture you think lies ahead doesn't matter and will never occur if you miss the small windows of opportunity before you every day. The line he likes to use is that "there are no neutral interactions." In other words, with every word, every nonverbal cue, every action, you leave each person you come across either a little better or a little worse. It's a tough pill to swallow, but Scanlon is dead on.

STRATEGY PLUS SPONTANEITY

Despite our best efforts to plan a safe and tidy path to growth, the greatest progress never occurs through strategy alone. To expand your potential, you must invite right-brained spontaneity into your left-brained strategy. Spontaneity alone is not a sustainable or viable strategy. But strategy without spontaneity is the quickest path to stagnation. It is the way of the machine—a path that unfortunately many companies take, making you a mere mechanical component that is greatly limited in potential.

A machine can do only what a machine was made to do. And each component of that machine can do only what it is designed to do, or it will not function properly. While certain parts are more critical than others—for instance, a cracked head gasket in a car engine is a more serious problem than a squeaky radiator fan—no part in a machine can expand its role without compromising the machine. This is why systematic executives love to preach execution. Do your job. The role is the role. Clearly defined, utterly static, restricting potential.

In the end, the parts in a machine don't have flexibility. The only variation in any mechanical part's role is to work faster or slower. It can't innovate.

A body is different from a machine.

While a body is also made up of moving parts that work together to produce a result, a body, unlike a machine, can produce an array of different products in a seemingly infinite combination of ways. That's because, unlike the parts of a machine, the parts of a body have significant flexibility.

The parts of a body can collaborate to sprint one hundred meters in under ten seconds, or climb Mount Everest over the course of a week, or achieve a couple of hours of rest in a hammock between two Caribbean palm trees. In short, the primary difference between a machine and a body is potential.

A machine and its parts are terminally limited by design.

A body and its parts are only temporarily limited by the effort and ingenuity of each part. That is where you come in.

Any single part of a body—any individual employee—
can expand the limits of what the body can do at any given
time. In this way, a body thrives off an undulating blend of
science and art, a potent combination of what is—led by
strategy—and what can still be—led by spontaneity.

We, as individuals and companies, tend to lean heavily on
strategy. But spontaneity is the better catalyst. Strategy alone
insulates us from our potential. Spontaneity removes the insulation to ensure that we remain exposed to possibilities we
never considered before. That requires a regular shock to the
system.

SHOCKING THE SYSTEM

One of the biggest challenges you face is resisting a mechanical
work environment, or what we call the "well-oiled machine."
If you do not resist the pull to fit in and simply do your part,
you will become a mechanical, perfunctory employee. The
domino effect continues as mechanical people in mechanical environments churn out predictable products, solutions,
and efforts. The obvious problem is that mechanical—that
is, predictable—is not inspiring to anyone along the value
chain—not you, not your colleagues, not your customers.

Like a sudden twist in a story, every company needs a
shock to the system now and then. Timing is important here.
Within every business there is context. Choosing the right
time to be spontaneous is key. If I am the unfortunate re-
cipient of quadruple bypass heart surgery, I don't want that
to be the time my surgeon embraces spontaneity and goes in

search of new creative incisions. I want her to use the same successful, homogenous approach she has used thousands of times before.

But don't make the mistake that every work endeavor is a quadruple bypass surgery. It's simply not.

There is regularly opportunity for you to toss out the old script and create a new one by asking why and how again. If you don't do this on a regular basis, you will become too predictable for your own good.

One of my favorite aspects of the Art Drops is when I get to witness what transpires afterward. Occasionally, when the venue is conducive to it, I will drop my painting in a location with a lot of foot traffic and then perch myself somewhere nearby with my phone camera inconspicuously aimed at the spot. What typically ensues is a study in human tendency to avoid unplanned conclusions.

I once dropped a large painting of Abraham Lincoln in plain view on the steps leading to the Lincoln Memorial in Washington, D.C. I then strolled about fifty meters away and sat on a bench. I watched as dozens of tourists walked by it, looked at it, talked about it, maybe wondered about why it was there, but never once suspected it to be a valuable piece of art they could take home and hang on their wall. They never once glanced at the back of the painting—which would have been easy since it was simply leaning against cement steps— where I always leave a message saying the painting is for finders to keep. Some bystanders even posed for pictures while sitting behind it.

These are the typical events that unfold immediately after an Art Drop, and before those who follow my Twitter and Facebook updates solve the mystery of the painting's location and show up to claim it. But every once in a while, a random passerby is brave enough to question the status quo and embrace some spontaneity—with a little help from the wind.

I was in Atlanta in 2011 to perform for a large corporate client there and, on the night before I was to take the stage, I created an original painting of Martin Luther King Jr. The next day, after my performance, I took a cab to the National Historic Site dedicated to the civil rights leader and leaned the painting against the outer wall of the Chapel of All Faiths, where I knew there would be foot traffic. I then found a place nearby to sit and observe.

As usual, several minutes passed while several tourists walked by, looked at the painting, snapped photos with it, and moved on. They treated the painting as if it were part of the memorial site—just as it appeared to be. But then a mother approached it with her small son and teenage daughter. The two kids took turns posing for pictures for their mom. Little Demarius, the son, posed last. But as he positioned himself next to the painting, a brief gust of wind blew the painting over on its face before his mom could snap the shot. Demarius looked down at the painting and slowly read the message on the back: "Congrats. You won an Art Drop. You found it. You keep it." His face lit up as his mom arrived to set the painting back up. He prompted her to read the message. I watched as her mouth fell open. She began looking around for someone to verify their discovery. Surely, it wasn't true; the painting appeared to be part of the site. But then again, my note said otherwise.

Reluctantly, the family began to tote away their prize, still looking around for someone to stop them and tell them it wasn't real. That's when I caught their eyes. I approached and introduced myself as the artist. I then confirmed their hopes. The painting belonged to Demarius. He found it; he got to keep it. They were speechless. But it was more than a lucky break. They earned the painting by embracing the spontaneity of a single moment.

EMBRACING MYSTERY

There is an interesting paradox at play when it comes to mystery in our own stories. While we are always inspired by the brilliant unveiling of creative potential in people like Choi Sung-Bong or Susan Boyle or Paul Potts, we are doubtful and largely resistant to the same unexpected twist in our own stories. Some of us even fool ourselves into thinking we are pursuing mystery when what we call spontaneity is nothing more than a calculated risk—the left brain trying to imitate the right brain.

Adding a little extra to Christmas bonuses or instituting casual Friday or sending personal birthday cards to customers is not embracing mystery. You've already thought through those scripts and know where they will lead. While you might tell yourself you're taking a chance, in truth you're only padding the insulation around your current stories. You're scripting mystery, which isn't mysterious at all and holds no hope of a great unveiling.

The 1995 film *First Knight* offers a good example of what

this looks like through the character Lancelot (played by Richard Gere). At face value, we take Lancelot to be a man full of passion—a rogue wanderer who unflinchingly seizes the greatest opportunities before him no matter the risk. A man unfazed by danger and mystery. We are drawn to his unbridled ways. But as we find out, there's more to Lancelot than meets the eye. Soon he meets King Arthur (played by Sean Connery), who discerns that he is really hiding his insecurities behind the facade of spontaneity and risk. In truth, he is utterly afraid to embrace the mystery of his full potential.

We pick up the story after Lancelot has just successfully run the Gauntlet, a medieval obstacle course, something that up to that point no one has ever done. Thoroughly impressed at Lancelot's feat, Arthur invites him into the castle to show him the famous Round Table. As Lancelot leans on the table, he reads the circular inscription.

LANCELOT: "In serving each other, we become free."

ARTHUR: That is the very heart of Camelot. Not these stones, timbers, towers, palaces. Burn them all, and Camelot lives on because it lives in us. It's a belief we hold in our hearts. *[Returns his sword to its sheath and exchanges a brief glance with Lancelot]* Well, no matter. Stay in Camelot; I invite you.

LANCELOT: *[Laughing]* Thank you. But I'll be on the road again soon.

ARTHUR: Oh? What road?

LANCELOT: Wherever chance takes me. I have no plans.

ARTHUR: So you believe that what you do is a matter of chance?

LANCELOT: *[Confidently]* Yes.

ARTHUR: *[Pointing]* Well, at the end of that hallway there are two doors—one to the left and one to the right. How will you decide which door to take?

LANCELOT: Left or right. Makes no difference. It's all chance.

ARTHUR: Then I hope chance leads you to the left because it's the only way out. *[Lancelot smiles, nods good-bye, and turns to leave]*

ARTHUR: Lancelot? *[Lancelot stops; turns to face Arthur as he continues speaking]* Just a thought . . . a man who fears nothing is a man who loves nothing. And if you love nothing, what joy is there in your life?

These are words that haunt Lancelot despite his efforts to shake them. They eventually break through the facade that is impeding his potential for greatness.

ON BEING SPONTANEOUS

King Arthur's words to Lancelot sum up the litmus test of spontaneity: fear. If you are truly being spontaneous, you will always fear something along the continuum from mild disappointment to complete disaster. However, the overlooked aspect of spontaneity is that it is anything but a chore. Spontaneity will stretch you, yes. But it is because you are stretched that it can be one of the most exhilarating and fulfilling things you do.

Ever jump off a cliff into a body of water? Even if you've done it numerous times, there is an element of fear that never leaves. But, oh, the exhilaration you feel once you've done it far outweighs the fear beforehand. There is a reason the term "adrenaline junkie" exists. The feeling on the backside of spontaneity is addictive. In fact being spontaneous exposes you to a degree of delight you may not have experienced since the wonder years of your childhood, when all bets were off every day because no script had yet been written.

We are delighted by spontaneity. And yet we frame our days by certainty.

We are inspired by mystery. And yet we pursue only paths that lead to known destinations.

Our left brains tell us that our days are easiest when we know what to expect. There's truth in that. But our right brains remind us that our days are inspiring only when we venture into the unknown. There's transcendence in that. The greatest stories contain both truth and transcendence.

To unveil your unknown potential, you must work with more than what is expected. You must also enter the realm of the unknown and unexpected.

Here's how.

1. Act Through the Fear

You might feel unfit for the mystery that lies ahead of you—even frightened at what you might find. Both feelings are normal. We are never fit for what we don't know—until we discover it. And nothing about the unknown is without some fear—but the adventure makes it worth it.

Remember that courage is not the absence of fear but the ability to move forward despite it. Don't attempt to think your way into acting spontaneously. Either you'll feign the act or you'll never move. Instead, act your way into thinking. Schedule that needed meeting with your boss even when you're not sure he'll buy into your idea. Tell that justifiably unhappy customer you'll waive the fee even when it's not your company's policy—then cover it with your own money if you can't find a way to get the policy changed. Agree to lunch with the new hire even though you have nothing in common—then explore for points of harmony. A few samplings of the rich rewards of spontaneity will whet your appetite for more. Just don't make the mistake of scripting your reward.

2. Leave Room for Interruptions

The problem with scripts is not that they don't work; it's that they do, in only one way. Don't get me wrong; scripted days are necessary for keeping momentum. But there are two effective ways to make progress:

- Take the road before you and keep the blinders on.
- Take the road before you and look for better roads.

The first way gets you where you expect to arrive when you expect to arrive there.

The second way also gets you where you expect to arrive when you expect to arrive there. The difference is that the second way is the only way that can potentially get you there sooner. It is also the only way you can arrive someplace even better.

This isn't merely a lesson in efficiency. It's a lesson in how to script your days without sabotaging your innovation potential.

Being creative is about connecting dots in ways they've never been connected before. There are infinite new possibilities, an incalculable number of potential combinations. Some of them are groundbreaking.

This is where tightly scripted days fail. They hold a deconstructive view of possibility. They assert, "There is nothing new that can come of today." No new connections, no new possibilities, no new innovations.

On the other hand, when your to-do list doesn't automatically rule out interruptions, you leave new possibilities on your list. That unexpected phone call . . . that impromptu meeting . . . that random interaction—all possess the potential to spark innovation. Use good judgment here. Playing solitaire is not a catalyst. Nor is tweeting a picture of your latest pair of kicks. If it keeps you honest, create a list of interruptions that possess possibility and that you will therefore consider fielding—things like requests for help from coworkers, unscheduled calls from clients, or impromptu conversations in the hall. Make room for them in your day.

There is a tendency to see spontaneity as frivolous or even careless behavior. "You can't just drop everything," the logic goes, "and go on a wild goose chase." This is a flawed view, and here's why. It assumes that you are happy with your current "everything."

If you are, stay the course and keep the blinders on. Entertain nothing new. Chase no mystery. Unearth no hidden potential.

If your everything isn't everything it's cracked up to be, drop it now and then and see what else you find. Mystery is at the heart of creativity. And spontaneity invites mystery.

Be spontaneous.

be surrendered

He is no fool who gives what he cannot keep to gain that which he cannot lose.

—JIM ELLIOT

On May 10, 1940, Winston Churchill became the prime minister of England as the country entered its ninth month in World War II. He felt the gravity of the moment. Things that might have traditionally mattered—things like pomp, protocol, and policy—didn't matter anymore. When he met his cabinet three days later, he told them, "I have nothing to offer but blood, toil, tears, and sweat." It was a message he would echo later the same day as he stood to deliver his first speech to the House of Commons.

There was no time for small talk. No time for pandering or punditry. What the country needed was to know what mattered most. Only from that footing could they move forward with confidence.

Churchill's speech was succinct, only four brief paragraphs when written. Yet it left no doubt about what would, as long as he held the brush, paint the canvas of England's future. The following summed up the message:

> *We have before us an ordeal of the most grievous kind. We have before us many, many long months of struggle and of suffering. You ask, what is our policy? I can say: It is to wage war, by sea, land and air, with all our might and with all the strength that God can give us; to wage war against a monstrous tyranny, never surpassed in the dark, lamentable catalogue of human crime. That is our policy. You ask, what is our aim? I can answer in one word: It is victory, victory at all costs, victory in spite of all terror, victory, however long and hard the road may be; for without victory, there is no survival.*[1]

What Churchill clarified was England's most fundamental why—that foundational thing for which she was willing to die, that one cause for which all other causes would be willingly surrendered if and when necessary. It is something you too must clarify for yourself if you are to realize your full creative potential.

YOUR BEST INSPIRATION FOR INNOVATION . . . IS YOU

The most important question you can ask about your work, and one of the most difficult to answer, is: Why do you do what you do?

It's a question you must answer—because if you don't, your workplace will do it for you.

I've met tens of thousands of business professionals over the past decade. The vast majority of them have the most honorable intentions. They truly want to be and do more. They desperately desire to rediscover their creative potential. They see the difference it will make. But they lack personal inspiration. And without it, they cannot move forward.

While your company's success might be an honorable motivator, especially if you are personally aligned with your company's mission statement, working for your company's sake is not enough. You have to discover that in the end you are working toward your own goals, and your company benefits from you. It's not the other way around.

We don't desire to be more innovative and inspirational to pad the company's P&L sheet. It's more personal than that. Unless you are the owner of the company, the "bottom line" is probably not even one of your top five reasons you want to be and do more at work.

Often, though, we never take the time to know what really is on that list for us. We are subsequently left with motivators like the company's profits and its statement of purpose—noteworthy factors but not personally moving factors—certainly not things you'd die for.

The truth is that to unearth your greatest catalyst for innovation, you have to forget your company and delve deep within your soul. You have to return to that childlike place where you dreamed about what you wanted to be when you grew up. Do you remember those dreams?

"As children, we wanted to be some*thing*—," writes best-selling author Todd Duncan in *Time Traps,* "a ballplayer, a ballerina, a doctor, a nurse, a lawyer, a teacher. . . . As teens we wanted to be some*one*. We were each the same something— a student—so what mattered most was acceptance, who we were seen to be. Popularity was more important than our place in the world. But then, sometime after high school, our wantings began to merge into a grander vision for our lives. We wanted to be both something and someone. And at the heart of that vision was a job."[2]

Duncan goes on to describe what then happens to most of us in the process of becoming that something and someone we dreamed we'd be. Over time, he says, our job becomes more than part of our identity; it becomes all of our identity. In our pursuit of meaningful work, in the pursuit of find-ing ourselves and flourishing in our jobs, we end up losing ourselves and wilting. The worst part is that most of us don't realize it's happened until we are so far removed from what originally inspired us that we barely remember what we hoped we would do and be.

Sometimes we need to remember what mattered first, not what matters right now. The tyranny of the urgent needs to be supplanted by the tyranny of the ultimate. What ulti-mately matters . . . to you?

Later in his tenure as England's fearless leader, Win-ston Churchill noted that at first we shape our life's work and then it shapes us. In the context in which he said it, Churchill was giving the positive side of the story: work makes us better people. Unfortunately, the other side of the story is more common. We choose our work to become the person we desire, but work then makes us people we never intended to be. Instead of us shaping it, it shapes us, often for the worse.

No matter what side of this journey you are currently on, you cannot escape that your work shapes you one way or the other. "Work is at the center of our lives and influences who we are and all that we do . . . ," writes Al Gini in *My Work, My Self.* "It is not just about getting paid, about gainful employment. Nor is it only about the use of one's mind and body to accomplish a specific task or project. Work is also one of the most significant contributing factors to one's inner life and development."[3]

For better or worse, concludes Gini, our work "not only provides us with an income, it literally names us, identifies us, to both ourselves and others." In other words, whether we like it or not, we are, in large part, what we do.

If your work identifies you, what does it say? That's where the why question comes in.

If you don't like what your work says about you today, then your job is shaping you without your permission.

On the other hand, if your inspiration is true, then you are actively participating in how your job shapes you.

The divergence between the two paths is not about what you do, it's about why you do it.

When you're asking yourself why you do what you do, there are pat answers and there are profound ones. We typically give the pat answers. They are the first to come to mind. They are also the logical answers. And so when we ask ourselves why we do what we do, we answer, "To pay the bills" or "To put food on the table."

Those aren't your deepest reasons for working. They won't inspire you to greater potential. They aren't the things for which you'd surrender all else—not in a First World country. This doesn't mean they aren't true needs. We all have to pay the bills and eat. But you don't stay up at night dreaming about dinner and utilities. They're not dreams you'd jot in a journal or keep in your wallet. They don't light a fire for breakthrough.

Then what does?

I can't answer that question. Only you can. Hopefully, you already did in the chapter on conviction. Let me offer a little reminder with a paraphrase of the Howard Thurman quote I mentioned in chapter 5: *Don't ask what your company needs. Ask yourself what makes you come alive. Because what your company needs is people who have come alive.*[4]

What makes you come alive is your why, no matter where you work or what your job description says you do. When you know this, the artist in you awakens and the tasks before you are painted in far more vibrant hues.

WHAT YOU SURRENDER

The truth is that you surrender something every day just as a painter surrenders each drop of paint on a canvas. That paint cannot be retrieved and the canvas is forever altered. Over time, a painting emerges. What that painting looks like is determined by the drops that were surrendered.

What do your drops look like?

All blue? ("I don't like my work.")

All pink? ("Hey, everybody, look at me!")

Or are they an eclectic mix of colors that offer a compelling picture of who you are deep down?

Your daily work is creating a painting, with or without your permission. The issue is whether it is a distinctive work of art worthy of hanging on the walls of the hearts and minds of family members, friends, and coworkers—or whether it is a cheap print that is reproduced ten thousand times a year and hung in office halls across the nation.

Whatever your painting looks like today, don't let your company or your job description determine where your drops of paint fall from here on out. You determine them. You determine what is surrendered to the canvas each day. Don't let your work become a picture someone else commissioned you to paint. Let it be your vision. Choose your colors. Paint them into a picture that moves you first and foremost. When it moves you, it will move others too. That's not necessarily because others will care about the same things you do. It is because everyone on the planet is moved by passion. Passion is the telltale sign of surrender, and it will distinguish your work as a work of art.

"All work contains drudgery," said the farmer-poet Wendell Berry; "the issue is whether it holds meaning or not."[5] No matter what it is you desire to accomplish though your work, no matter what you hope to create with your days, the measure of uniqueness and innovation you bring to your work will be in proportion to your surrender. I am not talking about bartering. True surrender is not a trade-off. It is an utter release, a depletion, a pouring out. While we cannot know or control the results of this release, like water poured onto a fertile field, passionate surrender always inspires growth.

Here's what I mean:

While on a trip to a remote village in Argentina in 2006, a Texan named Blake Mycoskie learned that many of the children there couldn't afford shoes. Since walking was the primary mode of transportation in the village, many of these children's feet suffered from a serious disease called podoconiosis that is contracted from bare feet coming into regular contact with soil rich in silicon dioxide. The debilitating disease was keeping many Argentine children from attending school. They were bound to their homes, unable to be educated or do the things that children love to do. The worst part was that podoconiosis is 100 percent preventable. When Mycoskie learned this, he surrendered to finding a solution.

He returned to the States, sold the online driver's education company he owned, and self-funded a new company that would manufacture a simple style of shoes based on the traditional Argentine *alpargata* design worn by farmers for centuries. For every pair he sold, he would give a pair away to a needy child in the remote village. In other words, his business model would include paying for the manufacturing, warehousing, and shipping of products that would never make a profit. There was something more important than maximizing revenue while minimizing overhead. There were children's lives to change.

Mycoskie launched his business, named TOMS, in the

States later that same year, and the response was explosive. In a matter of months, word of the TOMS vision spread, and people flocked to buy a pair of Mycoskie's shoes, not because they were the most exquisite ones available but because they were moved by the picture of passion—and compassion—they painted. They were moved by Mycoskie's surrender.

Since that first year, TOMS has expanded its output and its line of shoes but has remained true to its original vision. To date, TOMS has given away more than a million pairs of shoes and is recognized as one of the most innovative companies of the past decade.

ON SURRENDERING

The title of Blake Mycoskie's 2011 book, *Start Something That Matters,* sums up the message of true surrender.

Start today. And make sure what you start truly matters to you. You are going to surrender to something every day. Let it be something you deeply believe in. Let the canvas of your day be painted with the hues of your heart and soul.

And in the process of surrendering *to* the things that matter to you, here are four things you should expect to surrender *up* along the way.

1. Surrender the Recognition

In the business world, recognition is held high and lofty. Branding is the standard strategic ticket to it, whether we're talking about your self-brand or a company's brand. But we have to be careful we're not telling a story that isn't who we are, that is merely what our customers or coworkers want us to be or want to hear. The greatest businesses and business-people today are not known for their campaigns. They are known for their convictions, their commitments—in short, their consistent surrender that lets us know what matters to them. The irony is that today the strongest personal and corporate brands are not traditionally branded. They are recognized not because of their pleas for recognition but because of their determination to be led by their passionate actions rather than by their need for acknowledgment.

It is a challenge both in the marketplace and inside the walls of your company to resist the urge to campaign for others' praise. We want to be sure the boss knows the big idea was ours or the public knows how successful we've been. We want the credit because we fear without it we'll never receive our reward, whether it's a promotion or a simple "Good job" from the boss. But true surrender requires doing for the sake of being, not for the sake of being seen. "Let another man praise you, and not your own mouth," says the ancient proverb.[6]

The secret is that there's an unspoken promise with surrender. Your consistent actions will speak more loudly than clever or convincing words ever can. And when your passion is recognized apart from self-promotion, it will have a much further-reaching effect. But even if it doesn't, the other half of the secret is that by surrendering you will achieve simple, unadulterated peace in your heart and soul. To know that you have done all you can and have been who you were made to be is, in the long run, more valuable than any recognition another could give.

Be you, with passion. And surrender the recognition. Your daily mirror is recognition enough.

2. Surrender the Labels

Art is my channel, the medium that I've been given. It's what I'm most comfortable with, and it's where I don't get nervous. My art is where I relax and I create something the audience hasn't seen before, and it gives me the platform to have all this other stuff make sense. But I make a point to not get caught up in labels. It's a challenge in the world today because labels give us status.

The trouble is that they also bind us to rules.

Whether it's attorney, physician, Republican, Democrat, prolife, prochoice, Christian, Jew, Catholic, or atheist, once we define ourselves by those labels it is difficult to break free. We are tempted daily to pick up the paints that the label indicates we should, and to begin painting a canvas to match our label-mates.

An increasing illumination in my own life as an "artist" is to demystify the value of these self-imposed labels. If we are not careful, labels become conclusive and therefore limiting. This is an important point, since the book you hold in your hands seemingly purports to offer you a label you've probably not owned before.

While I want you to see that you are an artist, I also want

you to see that we all are. As far as I know, there is not a single living person who has only a left brain. We all have the capacity to be artists, so the "artist" label is no label at all. It is a synonym for *human,* and that is the nonlabel that unites us all. This is the point: unity, collaboration, compassion.

When we surrender our labels and the rules that come with them, we are suddenly open to all fields of possibility. Pat Tillman is a prime example.

In the aftermath of 9/11, the world watched as a hard-hitting, highly respected professional football player named Pat Tillman surrendered the label of professional athlete, turning down a multimillion-dollar contract with the Arizona Cardinals to serve his country. Tillman enlisted in the army in June 2002, subsequently rose through the ranks, and in 2003 became a member of the Army Rangers. Approximately a year later, Tillman was tragically killed in Afghanistan by friendly fire.

Much has been said about the man who surrendered money and prestige to die for something he believed in more. But perhaps most amazing about Tillman is that what he believed in wasn't the war. The grandson of a Pearl Harbor survivor, he believed in his duty to a country his family and friends had fought and died for. This "why" moved him to forgo millions and enter into a fight he spoke openly against among family and friends, insisting all along that he did not want to be used as a public relations prop.

Pat Tillman clearly did not care about labels. As a result, he was, according to close friend and former teammate Jake Plummer, "one of the freest thinking guys I've ever been around. . . . That was the beauty of that guy. He just had a very unique perspective on things. He was a one of a kind."[7]

He was surrendered to his own art.

3. Surrender the Moment

The most recognizable line from Martin Luther King Jr.'s most famous speech on the steps of the Lincoln Memorial is undoubtedly "I have a dream . . ." But according to *Time* magazine, perhaps the most significant line of his speech was this: "We have also come to this hallowed spot to remind America of the fierce urgency of Now. This is no time to engage in the luxury of cooling off or to take the tranquilizing drug of gradualism. Now is the time to make real the promises of democracy."[8]

Now is a powerful word, one of the most powerful words in the world. It is also a frightening word because it leaves no room for another ounce of planning. Yet it is the only aspect of time that we can control. Your past is written in stone. Your future is not guaranteed, not even the end of today. What you have in your possession is this moment with this book in your hand. With this moment, you can affirm all you have been and mark it down as a day like the rest—an expected, typical day. Or you can use it to change, to improve, to break out of a common and mechanical mold.

What you do with now is all you can do. Surrender your now to the things that matter most to you. Surrender your now to the artist in you.

4. Surrender the Outcome

Forbes contributor Steven Kotler recently wrote about the lesser-known connection between Einstein's genius and his willingness to take enormous risks. As a prime example he cites a great incongruity in Einstein's life: he was an avid sailor, and he didn't know how to swim. Not only that, explains Kotler, "He often took unnecessary chances while sailing. For the years that he summered in Nassau Point (1937–1939) . . . rumor has it that he occasionally delighted in sailing unsuspecting scientists directly into storms—for the sheer fun of it."[9]

The point this makes, says Kotler, is that "there is a deep and meaningful connection between surrender and creativity."

"Begin with the end in mind" has been a commandment of the corporate world for a couple of decades. But is it sound advice? No, not when your focus is so result oriented that you lose sight of the joy in the journey. We've all experienced this dynamic, if not during a road trip, certainly in hindsight after one. We spent weeks obsessing about the destinations. Then we hopped in the car and pressed the gas pedal, only to realize, somewhere in the middle of Utah, that the drive from one destination to the next was as much fun, if not more fun, than each arrival.

"Life is what happens to you while you're busy making other plans," sang John Lennon.[10] Enjoy your daily journey at work—relish the unexpected humor, adventure, and beauty of your interactions and regular duties—and the monthly outcomes will often take care of themselves.

SURRENDER TO CREATIVITY

Rediscovering and reactivating the artist in you will not occur apart from surrender. But that's often easier said than done. Surrender will come less naturally the more ingrained you are in your ways and the more comfortable you are in your current state. Often the more threatened we are by a change in our routine—the more cynical we become about our future—the less creative we can be. Older folks have trouble here. But some of us younger bucks act just as old if we're not mindful—a point the noted author Anaïs Nin made to a seventeen-year-old aspiring author who was having trouble with surrender:

> Older people fall into rigid patterns. Curiosity, risk, exploration are forgotten by them. You have not yet discovered that you have a lot to give, and that the more you give the more riches you will find in yourself. It amazed me that you felt that each time you write a story you gave away one of your dreams and you felt the poorer for it. But then you have not thought that this dream is planted in others, others begin to live it too, it is shared, it is the beginning of friendship and love. . . .
>
> You must not fear, hold back, count or be a miser with your thoughts and feelings.[11]

All great creativity is bound to surrender. It begins with who you are and what you have that matters most, and from those two things you create something worthy of pouring out for others. Then, as an empty vessel, you go back to work filling yourself back up with more of the things that matter, more of the emotions and experiences and lessons of your days, so that you will again have the material to create another work of art worthy of pouring out. This filling up and pouring out never stops when you are an artist. It takes constant courage. But courage and surrender are what make creations so beautiful.

No enduring work of art has ever come from cowardice and greed. Be bold enough to be you. And courageous enough to give yourself away each day.

Be surrendered.

9

be original

Everyone has his own specific vocation or mission in life . . . Therein he cannot be replaced, nor can his life be repeated. Thus, everyone's task is as unique as is his specific opportunity to implement it.

—Viktor Frankl

You have one advantage over every other person on the planet: you are the only you. No one brings the same combination of experience, humor, skill, personality, and presence to the world. But *being* you is one thing—you cannot escape the man in the mirror. The real goal is *doing* you by expressing your uniqueness in your work and what you produce. We have to fight to be ourselves every day, to fight against the dominating force of homogenization.

In the 1950s, Swarthmore University psychologist Solomon Asch performed a series of now-famous experiments that showed how shockingly willing our minds are to go with the crowd when introduced to peer pressure. It also shows us what we have to fight against in order to remain true to our originality.[1]

For Asch's experiments, groups of six to eight students were assembled and informed that they were participating in a vision test. All but one student, however, were co-conspirators with Asch in the experiment and had been coached in how to proceed.

Each round began with the group of students seated at the same table or two rows of tables and facing Asch. The psychologist showed them a white poster board with a single, vertical line on the left side of a certain length, and three vertical lines on the right side labeled 1, 2, and 3 or A, B, and C. Of the three lines on the right, one was shorter, one was longer, and one was the same length as the line on the left. The object of the so-called vision test was to choose which of the three lines to the right matched the length of the line on the left. The correct answer was obvious every time.

After being shown the first poster board, the students were asked one at a time to verbalize which of the three lines to the right (1, 2, or 3) matched the single line to the left. The conspirators answered first and the one test subject answered last. In the first two trials, the conspirators all verbalized the correct answer and the test subject followed suit. But Asch had prepared a twist in the third trial.

Upon seeing the third poster board, the conspirators had all been instructed to choose the same incorrect answer, which they did. The main question was: What would the test subject do? Over the course of the entire experiment, the students were shown a total of eighteen poster boards, and the conspirators verbalized the same incorrect answer twelve times. Asch assumed the test subjects would not conform to something so obviously incorrect. He was wrong.

Asch ran the experiment 123 times. When the results were combined, incredibly, only 25 percent of the test subjects did not conform on any trial, while 75 percent conformed at least once and there was an average of 37 percent conformity per experiment. In other words, the test subjects conformed to the obvious wrong answer more than one-third of the time.

To be certain the results were not an issue of poor vision or the lines being too small, Asch's control groups in which no conspirators were present were asked to write down their answers individually instead of verbalizing them for everyone else to hear. They chose the correct-length line 98 percent of the time, indicating that the incorrect answers were indeed a result of the desire to go along with the crowd.

Finally, Asch wondered about the effect that the number of people present in the group would have on conformity— namely the number of conspirators. Interestingly, when just one conspirator was present, there was virtually no impact on test subjects' answers. The presence of two conspirators had only a small effect. However, when three or more conspirators were present, the effect was far more significant, bringing to mind the proverb that "a cord of three strands is not quickly broken."[2]

When the test subjects were interviewed after each experiment and asked why they had made the choices they made, a small percentage admitted that peer pressure affected their choices approximately one-quarter of the time. However, the majority confessed that they weren't sure why they made the choices they made—many simply weren't aware they were choosing the wrong answer.

Are we really so naive that we aren't even aware of the extent to which we follow the crowd?

Are you truly unaware that you don't follow your own voice but instead choose to echo the voices of others?

THE ENEMY OF ORIGINALITY

Given that work environments are far more hectic and stressful than Asch's lab, the pressure to conform is far greater. The need for results is driven into you from day one, and it often makes the most logical sense to simply look around at what others are doing and fall in line.

Or, at the very least, we don't stick out like a sore thumb. We fit in.

What happens, though, when you are presented with a new challenge, one that can't be solved by old processes and simply following the pack? When you are asked to come up with the direction for the new marketing campaign and present it at the executive meeting? When you are asked to streamline the sales process and reduce overhead? When your manager asks you to lead the next quarterly planning meeting? What then?

Sure, you could still ask around and gather some intelligence on precedents that have been set. That may work. But it will not make you a greater asset to your company. And it will not add greater meaning to your days.

What will make you a success and bring meaning is painting your work with your special brush—your personality and convictions. That's the essence of being original.

Do you remember the Microsoft employee Fred Jordan from earlier in the book? He was tasked with finding a way to reduce the cost of delivering software to his company's biggest clients. He hit his head against a wall for weeks trying to come up with a big idea. He read articles, searched the Web, asked teammates for ideas. But nothing came of it: nothing he could confidently stand behind and present to his bosses. Fred was at a loss—until he considered what was meaningful to him. It turned out to be something that was meaningful to a lot of customers as well.

His breakthrough idea not only saved his customers and his company a ton of money, it earned Fred a promotion to a position that gives him even more creative space to paint his daily duties with personal meaning.

Why is it so difficult for us to resist the tug of conformity?

While our tendency is to point to fear as the culprit—fear of rejection, fear of being ostracized, fear of failure—it turns out that fear is not the only enemy of originality. False perception is also to blame.

You and I have an incredible ability to see things not as they are but as we want them to be.

In 2005, Emory University neuroscientist Dr. Gregory Berns and his research team mimicked Asch's 1950s study, using 3-D shapes for comparison instead of the lines. The objective remained the same, as did the method of testing. There was only one addition—an fMRI scanner to see what was actually going on in the brains of the conformers. Perhaps, Berns figured, it would give insight into why the conformity happened.

The results of Berns's experiments were the same as Asch's—a surprisingly high degree of conformity to the conspirators' wrong answers. When asked why they had conformed, the test subjects once again couldn't explain it. While they figured peer pressure had something to do with it, by and large the test subjects didn't feel it played a major role.

The fMRI data told a different story.

In his insightful *Psychology Today* article titled "Creativity: The Secret Behind the Secret," author and journalist Steven Kotler explains, "When subjects studied the shape, there was activation in the visual processing regions of the brain. . . . This was baseline data—exactly what we'd expect to see. But when subjects conformed, something else occurred. The parietal cortex, which before had emitted a faint glow, was now lit up like a Christmas tree—the telltale sign of hard work being done."[3]

Berns, in his book *Iconoclast,* offers an explanation for the "hard work" that occurred in the brains of the conforming test subjects. The group's wrong answers imposed a virtual image in the subject's brain that literally "beat out the image originating from the subject's own eyes."[4]

The effect?

The subject disregarded his or her own perception in order to conform to the group's perception.

"Berns's data," writes Kotler, "showed that conformity was also a perceptual problem—our brain literally showed us 'false' data when that terror [of nonconformity] began to grip us."

You've heard about talking yourself out of doing something. This is something entirely different. We're talking about you perceiving yourself out of something.

In essence, the pull to fit in with the crowd is so strong that it can literally change our brain's ability to think an original thought. Forget doing something original. If we can't even think originally, how is our unique bent ever going to escape our minds? How do we overcome this propensity to effectively fool ourselves into stuffing our originality?

While we can certainly work on thickening our skin or taking a detached approach to others' opinions or being more courageous individuals, these are neither the shortest nor the simplest paths. The quickest path to maintaining originality is to either see things differently than others or see different things. "The real voyage of discovery," said Marcel Proust, "lies not in seeking new landscapes but in seeing with new eyes."

The fact is that original breakthroughs rarely occur in places with which we are familiar. This includes the places in our own minds where we carry our preconceived notions about the people and places around us and where current knowledge resides.

In *Iconoclast,* Berns tells the story of preeminent glassblower Dale Chihuly, whose smallest bowls command a couple of thousand dollars and whose largest installations, like the one he did for the Bellagio Hotel in Las Vegas, command more than $1 million today. His breakthrough is one that tangibly illustrates what it takes to be original. It begins in the 1970s.

If you were a glassblower then, as Chihuly was, you knew

that the symmetry of your pieces was tantamount to success. From the very first blown glass invented by the Venetians in the thirteenth century, the measure of artistry for every glassblower was his steady-handed ability to produce a vase or bowl or lamp that was perfectly proportioned: perfect circle or oval or well-balanced design. Even after six centuries, explains Berns, "it was unthinkable to show work that departed from this standard. Asymmetric vases were the mark of rank beginners."[5] And so Chihuly's work followed protocol. Symmetrical. Balanced. Nothing unexpected.

That's not to say his work didn't have unique elements. At the time he was working at the Rhode Island School of Design, trying to merge Navajo blanket designs into glass sculptures, to no avail. The tools at his disposal would not hold the shapes, at least symmetrically. Instead, he ended up figuring a way to transfer the Navajo designs and other drawings onto the surface of the glass, like an etching. It added a little flair to his pieces, but in the end they were nothing special. The shapes were merely symmetrical cylinders that looked like candleholders. Clearly, Chihuly was a freethinker, but he had not broken through.

Then a car accident changed his vision, both physically and creatively.

During a tour of Great Britain in 1976, Chihuly was in a serious car accident in which he was thrown through the windshield, causing irreparable damage to his left eye. He began wearing a black patch over the blind eye. The new look took some adjustment from an emotional standpoint, but it was the physical adjustment to not having peripheral vision to one side or accurate depth perception that proved the bigger challenge. It also proved to be the critical catalyst that brought out the true artist in Chihuly.

While recovering, he felt handicapped with his limited vision but continued to blow glass with his team at the school of design. He pressed forward for nearly a year, making no significant strides, continually frustrated by the limits of his sight. Eventually, he was forced to consider a new way of working. Because the team worked in such close quarters, a scenario that required clear vision and accurate depth perception, neither of which Chihuly possessed, he made the decision to hand over his position of gaffer, the person who holds and rotates the pipe on which the glass is blown.

The decision opened up a new frontier.

No longer did Chihuly have to sit on a bench in close proximity to each piece of glass. Suddenly, he was able to view the pieces from all angles throughout the process and instruct team members at crucial moments to add more color or speed up the rotation or tilt the angle of the pipe. Suddenly, from this vantage point, the possibilities of what could be crafted were limitless.

The results, utterly asymmetrical and otherworldly, were so mind-blowing and rare that in a matter of months their presence in the market began to tear down the six-hundred-year-old paradigm of symmetry, piece by unbalanced piece. The destruction today is complete. "Not since Louis Tiffany," concludes Berns, "has there been a force in glass like Chihuly."

THE EFFECT OF AN ORIGINAL PERSPECTIVE

The key question when it comes to being original is not one of form: What should my original work look like? The key question is one of perception: Who do you perceive yourself to be?

At first, Dale Chihuly saw himself as a mere gaffer—the man who blows the glass. From that perspective, his job was to follow the path glassblowers had taken for six centuries. If he was a glassblower, he needed to create works according to the existing rules of great glassblowing. Symmetry was king.

When Chihuly lost sight in his left eye, he could finally see that he was something more than a glassblower. Something bigger. He was an artist, an innovator, a groundbreaker.

From this perspective, he was not responsible to an established paradigm. He was free to create his own art, to innovate his craft, to break new ground. It made all the difference.

Are any "accepted" paradigms standing in the way of how you'd really love to work? Certain hours you're expected to be "on"? Certain days you're expected to be available? Certain ways you're expected to carry out tasks that just don't jibe with who you are inside?

If why you do what you do has more to do with being compliant than living your convictions, it's time to unthink how you work and create an original workplace paradigm, even if it's only for you. There are times when reframing your perspective about work is the only way to take your results to their highest creative potential. An important part of that new frame is defining yourself as an artist in your own right. Here's what I mean.

In 1978, the late educator and philosopher Mortimer Adler wrote an insightful book that brought to light the ancient Greek definition of an artist. It is freeing in its scope and confirms an aspect of the core message of this book— that we are all artists if we maintain the right perspective.

In *Aristotle for Everyone,* Adler explains that the ancient philosopher's understanding of art and subsequent definition of artistry were derived from the Greek word *techné,* which Aristotle used to describe the unique ability certain people have for making things that improve the well-being of themselves and others. "In Latin," explains Adler, "this becomes 'ars' and in English 'art.' An artist therefore is a person who has the technique, skill or know-how for making things."[6]

In other words, according to the ancient Greeks, art was a function not of eccentricity, or an aesthetic standard, or a certain industry-specific paradigm. Art was simply a function of making something unique and useful—the more unique and useful the better. That is one half of the coin.

ART THROUGH DESTRUCTION

Art is clearly about creation. But it is also about destruction. The title of Gregory Berns's book I mentioned earlier, *Iconoclast,* has significant meaning. The origin of the word is the Greek word *eikonoklastes,* which means "a destroyer of images." When Berns chose to name the most groundbreaking creatives in recent memory "iconoclasts," he was pointing not only to their unique creations but also to the destructive nature of what they created. In short, their creations blew up the stale standards of the status quo in their companies and often their industries as well. They demolished expectations. This, too, is part of being an original artist.

In some cases, artists literally abolish decades-long, even centuries-long, paradigms in order to forge an original, and better, way. They don't do this because they merely want to be helpful or useful. They also don't do this because they are merely compelled to be different—countercultural for the sake of being countercultural. They do this because they are compelled to create works that embody a perspective they hold dear. That doesn't always line up with current perspectives.

This isn't to say that to be original you must obliterate the status quo in your company. It simply means you must offer you, at your truest, and accept that it may confront a precious paradigm.

While a battle to the death may ensue, it is highly unlikely. More often than not, the opposite occurs. When presented with a better way or a truer perspective, life ensues. Freedom ensues. In your company. In your workdays. And in every aspect of your life. We call these "aha moments" or epiphanies. They always originate in someone—from there they can spread like wildfire.

ON BEING ORIGINAL

"The man who follows the crowd, will usually get no further than the crowd. The man who walks alone is likely to find himself in places no one has ever been before. . . . You have two choices in life: you can dissolve into the mainstream, or you can be distinct. To be distinct you must be different. To be different, you must strive to be what no one else but you can be."

It's a brilliant and fitting quote attributed to Alan Ashley-Pitt, a man who didn't exist. One of the finest quotes on originality was actually originated by a Santa Barbara–based greeting card company in the late 1960s, which created the name for attribution on their products.

It's a great picture of the long-term effect of an original perspective, no matter where it comes from. Here's how to ensure that your original works have the same staying power.

1. Dance to Your Own Drum

In Sir Ken Robinson's book *The Element,* he tells the story of an eight-year-old girl named Gillian who was struggling with her schoolwork and having difficulty staying focused in the classroom.[7] The problem escalated to the point that Gillian's attention problems became a constant disruption to her teachers and classmates. The school's top brass called her parents in to discuss a solution. They agreed to take Gillian to a psychologist.

When Gillian and her mother arrived, the psychologist asked the little girl to wait in his office while he talked with her mother in the hall. As he was stepping out of his office, he reached across his desk and turned on the radio.

As soon as they were in the hallway, the psychologist leaned over to Gillian's mother and said, "Just stand here for a moment, and watch what she does." Together, the two adults stood to one side and peered through a window into the doctor's office.

Gillian had risen to her feet and was gliding around the room to the music. But this was no ordinary childlike dance. Her movements were graceful, special, as if she knew precisely what she was doing. And her face was full of joy.

The two adults watched for a couple of moments, transfixed by Gillian, until finally the psychologist turned to Gillian's mother and said, "Gillian isn't sick. She's a dancer. Take her to a dance school."

Her mother did, and it would change Gillian Lynne's life forever. A few years later, she joined the Royal Ballet School in London, with which she traveled the world. Then one day she met a man named Andrew Lloyd Webber, and together they created three pieces you may have heard of: *Cats, Aspects of Love,* and *The Phantom of the Opera.*

We are all more than meets the eye—even our own eyes. We just have to believe it. Find that beat inside you, and then have the courage to dance to it every day, despite what others say.

2. Work Boldly, Uniquely, and Freely

We possess hundreds of original thoughts from the context of our own experience each day. The artistry comes in learning how and when to apply them, and then freeing yourself from the fear that holds you back from being your original self. What is it that we really fear? Failure? Sure. Rejection? Possibly. But I believe if you were honest—if any of us were honest—we would have to confess that regret is worse than both: the regret of a meaningless existence in which we did not pursue the things that fascinated us, inspired us, and brought us joy. "Conformity," said John F. Kennedy, "is the jailer of freedom and the enemy of growth."

The art inside you is like a bay window to greater significance. Peer into it and you will see that a world of possibility is available to you. Your challenge is that the same bay window—your original art—is flanked by large drapes of fear and conformity. When you are weak or overcome, you will be tempted to pull the drapes. It will feel safer not to look. You will think it removes the pangs. But it never really does.

No matter how weak you feel, look anyway. Don't try to ignore the art inside you—even if what you see scares you to death. You are not alone.

Consider the British writer G. K. Chesterton's reply to the London *Times*'s invitation to write an essay titled "What's Wrong with the World?"[8]

Chesterton's response:

Dear Sirs,
I am.
   Sincerely,
   G. K. Chesterton

Chesterton was a highly accomplished man. According to Irish playwright George Bernard Shaw, he was "a man of colossal genius."[9] Contemporaries from Oscar Wilde to H. G. Wells to C. S. Lewis were regularly engaged by his writings. It is said that his novel *The Man Who Was Thursday* inspired the revolutionary Irish republican leader Michael Collins, and his column in the *Illustrated London News* profoundly affected Mahatma Gandhi.[10]

If anyone could have provided a grand and eloquent solution to the question "What is wrong with the world?" it was Chesterton. But that would have been predictable. And we wouldn't be talking about it today. Instead, he looked inside himself and offered the truth he saw there. As it turned out, it was far more than an individual truth.

That is the strength of what's inside you. It is more potent than a single dose. "If you were meant to cure cancer or write a symphony or crack cold fusion and you don't," asserts author Steven Pressfield in *The War of Art,* "you not only hurt yourself, even destroy yourself; you hurt your children. You hurt me. You hurt the planet. Creative work is not a selfish act or a bid for attention on the part of the actor. It's a gift to the world and every being in it. Don't cheat us of your contribution. Give us what you've got."[11]

Don't cheat yourself. Don't cheat us. Give your world what you've got.

3. Recruit an Ally

When you were a child, you were largely unconscious of what other people thought. In fact, you were often oblivious to the presence of others standing right next to you. This oblivion was a catalyst to the growth of your knowledge, character, and creativity. You did what came naturally, and there was no filter between your mind and mouth. Over time you lost that glorious oblivion. Failures, expectations of others, cultural etiquette—they all carried one common message: be restrained. Don't show your hand or you'll get burned. People will laugh. You'll get in trouble. You won't be liked.

Unfortunately, the restraint you learned is only a step from stationary. And at work, stationary will get you nowhere. One simple way to get around the temptation to be restrained is to recruit an ally, someone who shares the same perspective. Not only will this boost your confidence in expressing your ideas or altering how you work, it can initiate a groundswell of support if you are really on to something special.

Don't wait for the big numbers before doing your artistic thing. But if you're having trouble resisting the urge to stay comfortable and conform, find a partner who will go forward with you. Sometimes two artists are better than one.

No matter what you've done or said to this point, it's time you stop asking what your job requires you to think or what your company asks you to believe. Those are predefined, finite parameters. Within those walls you cannot become anything more than an efficient company clone. Within those walls you cannot produce anything more than the products the system is set up to spit out.

Instead, ask yourself what you believe and who you long to be.

Now go be those in word and deed. Not when it's convenient. Not when it is proven to be dollar productive. Not when you are certain it will give you success. Go be those things today and every day thereafter because, as Einstein said, "There are only two ways to live your life. One is as though nothing is a miracle. The other is as though everything is a miracle."

Miracles are inside you and around you every day, waiting to be discovered. The question is not whether they are there. The question is whether you will see and seize them in a way only you can.

Open up the eyes of your heart and mind. Together they compose a mirror of who you truly are: an original artist with immense power to tear down the tired, old ways of working and replace them with methods that are meaningful— methods that will produce the environment and the products that matter most. Be the artist who originates the process. Then stay the course. You may be the only one who can.

your picasso

*My mother said to me, "If you are a soldier, you
will become a general. If you are a monk, you
will become the Pope." Instead, I was a painter,
and became Picasso.*

—Pablo Picasso

Before Dorothy and Toto entered
the story, the Tin Man had once been a human
lumberjack. He lived in the Munchkin village and fell
in love with a Munchkin girl who was a slave of the
Wicked Witch of the East. The Wicked Witch eventually grew worried that the lumberjack would take
the Munchkin slave away, so she put a curse on his ax.
Each time he went to chop a piece of wood, the ax
would slip and instead cut off a piece of his body.

Piece by piece, his body fell apart and the only way
he could carry on was to allow the tinsmith in the village to replace the severed body parts with artificial
limbs made of tin. Eventually, the lumberjack's body
was made entirely of tin—his heart included. The only

way he could continue on was with an oilcan to keep from being stiffened from rust. The other problem was that with a tin heart, the Tin Man could no longer love the Munchkin girl whom he was engaged to marry. And so he set out on a journey to find a heart and rediscover the man he had once been.

It's a parable that describes the process of rediscovering the artist in you. A journey we've now framed in full.

The path is laid out before you. But this is only a book, and these are only words on a page.

Unless they infect your daily life, unless they alter the way you work and remind you of what matters most, they are no more than wet paints sitting in puddles on a palette that I've presented to you. Wait to use them and they will eventually dry up. The only remnant you'll have of the emotions you felt and the vows you made as you read these pages are dried puddles of what could have been.

Don't let your paints dry. Use them immediately. Now. And if you are not yet comfortable with a brush, use your hands.

Before I had any inkling of the artist I am today, before I knew how to use a brush and palette properly, I dipped my fingers and hands in color and spread them across a large blank canvas until it was filled with unlikely combinations of colors, unexpected patterns, and unpredictable shapes. It was a liberating release. But it was also something more.

That blank canvas symbolized me at that point in my career. I was starting over. All was unknown. But anything was possible.

It was a frightening prospect standing there staring at the colorless canvas. But something inside me knew I had a choice—*the* choice of my career. There were three options.

1. I could keep staring at the blankness of the canvas and let fear and anxiety keep me from ever attempting anything new.

2. I could sit down at a desk and try to plan out what I'd like to make that canvas look like over the next year, five years, and ten years.

3. I could thrust my hands in paint and slap them on the canvas with every honest emotion I felt at that moment—frustration, anger, fear, hope, longing, wonder, gratitude, and anticipation—and see what resulted.

You now know I chose the third option.

Since then I've come to understand that the first blank canvas was not just a symbol of my career in that season of losing my job. It was a symbol of my career every day. And that choice—*the* choice—is something I am asked to make today, tomorrow, and every day I am given to work.

I choose to get my hands dirty and color the canvas as only I can.

I choose to take responsibility for the painting my days are creating.

I choose to be:

Provocative
Intuitive
Convicted
Accelerated
Spontaneous
Surrendered
Original

I hope you do too. Not just today and tomorrow, while the enthusiasm of this moment is still fresh. Not just in a right-brained, emotional, throw-caution-to-the-winds sort of way. In a left-brained, logical, this-is-my-ticket-to-freedom sort of way too.

You are a one-of-a-kind artist, capable of producing a one-of-a-kind work of art, every day. Be a whole artist. Mind and heart. Logic and emotion. Strategy and soul. Do that, and in no time you will have created your Picasso.

next step

Descartes said, "I think therefore I am."
I say, "I unthink therefore I create."

To continue your creative journey, I invite you to leverage your existing talents by better understanding the current creative skills you already possess. You might be surprised. Log on to www.theartofvision.com/unthink to take the creativity strengths test.

notes

Chapter 1

1. Tim Seldin, "Children Are Little Scientists: Encouraging Discovery Plan," n.d., http://childdevelopmentinfo.com/child-development/children-little-scientists.shtml.
2. Kaomi Goetz, "How 3M Gave Everyone Days Off and Created an Innovation Dynamo," n.d., www.fastcodesign.com/1663137/how-3m-gave-everyone-days-off-and-created-an-innovation-dynamo.
3. Glenn Llopis, *Earning Serendipity: 4 Skills for Creating and Sustaining Good Fortune in Your Work* (Austin, TX: Greenleaf Book Group, 2008).
4. Goetz, "How 3M Gave Everyone Days Off and Created an Innovation Dynamo."
5. Matthew 9:14 (*New International Bible,* 2011).
6. Ronald W. Clark, *Einstein: The Life and Times* (1971; repr., New York: Avon Books, 1984), 27–28.
7. Albert Einstein, *Cosmic Religion: With Other Opinions and Aphorisms* (New York: Covici-Friede, 1931), 97.
8. Walter Isaacson, "20 Things You Need to Know About Einstein," *Time,* April 5, 2007.
9. Outward Bound, "History," 2010, www.outward-bound.org/about/history.html.
10. Scott Thorpe, *How to Think Like Einstein: Simple Ways to Break the Rules and Discover Your Hidden Genius* (Naperville, IL: Sourcebooks, 2000), 5–6.

11. Ibid.

12. Jack Uldrich, *Jump the Curve: 50 Essential Strategies to Help Your Company Stay Ahead of Emerging Technologies* (Avon, MA: Platinum Press, 2008), quoted in "Think Like a Child," *Success,* November 4, 2009, www.success.com/articles/890-think-like-a-child.

13. Ibid.

14. Christopher Fry, *A Sleep of Prisoners* (Oxford: Oxford University Press, 1951).

15. Roy H. Williams, "5 Ways to Solve Problems Creatively," *Monday Morning Memo,* August 20, 2012, www.monday morningmemo.com/newsletters/read/1995.

Chapter 2

1. Edgar Lee Masters, *Spoon River Anthology* (New York: Signet Classics, 2007), quoted in John Eldredge, *Wild at Heart: Discovering the Secret of a Man's Soul* (Nashville, TN: Thomas Nelson, 2001), 210.

2. Debra Jennings, "Use Your Whole Brain: Leveraging Right-Brained Thinking in a Left-Brained World," n.d., www.projectsmart.co.uk/use-your-whole-brain-leveraging-right-brained-thinking-in-a-left-brained-world.html.

3. Alison Gopnik, quoted in "Think Like a Child," *Success,* November 4, 2009, www.success.com/articles/890-think-like-a-child.

4. "Too Much Knowledge Can Be Bad for Some Types of Memory, Study Finds," *ScienceDaily,* May 17, 2005, www.sciencedaily.com/releases/2005/05/050517112349.htm.

5. Jeffrey Davis, "Think Like a 47-Year-Old to Boost Creativity," *Tracking Wonder,* July 14, 2010, www.psychologytoday.com/blog/tracking-wonder/201007/think-47-year-old-boost-your-creativity.

6. Masters, *Spoon River Anthology,* quoted in Eldredge, *Wild at Heart.*

7. Daniel Pink, *A Whole New Mind: Why Right-Brainers Will Rule the Future* (New York: Riverhead Books, 2005).

Chapter 3

1. Anthony DeCurtis, "John Lennon: Biography," n.d., www.johnlennon.com/biography.
2. See the website Digital by Choice, www.digitalbychoice.com/en-us/.
3. "IBM 2010 Global CEO Study: Creativity Selected as Most Crucial Factor for Future Success," IBM news release, May 18, 2010, www-03.ibm.com/press/us/en/pressrelease/31670.wss.
4. Ibid.
5. Roy H. Williams, "5 Ways to Solve Problems Creatively," *Monday Morning Memo,* August 20, 2012, www.mondaymorningmemo.com/newsletters/read/1995.
6. Esther Jeles shared this story with Dale Carnegie & Associates in the book *How to Win Friends and Influence People in the Digital Age* (New York: Simon & Schuster, 2011). It has been told here with her permission. Jeles's services can be found at the following website: www.ayletinc.com.
7. Amy Jo Martin, *Renegades Write the Rules* (New York: Crown Business, 2012).

Chapter 4

1. Glenn Llopis, *Earning Serendipity: 4 Skills for Creating and Sustaining Good Fortune in Your Work* (Austin, TX: Greenleaf Book Group, 2008).
2. John Naisbitt, *Megatrends* (New York: HarperCollins, 1988).
3. Malcolm Gladwell, "Malcolm Gladwell on Intuition," interview by Samuel Greengard, *PM Network,* October 1, 2011, www.pmnetwork-digital.com/pmnetwork/201110/?pg=82.
4. Gladwell, "Malcolm Gladwell on Intuition."
5. Special thanks to Second City president Diana Martinez for

her insight regarding the creative genius of Neva Boyd and Viola Spolin and the beginnings of improvisation.

6. While this quote is widely attributed to Richard Feynman, the original source in which it was printed is unknown.

Chapter 5

1. Michelle Woo, "Dave Gibbons Is a Church Misfit," *OC Weekly,* September 8, 2011, www.ocweekly.com/2011-09-08/news/newsong-dave-gibbons/.

2. Jeremy Quittner, "Influencing People in the Digital Age," *Inc.,* October 24, 2012, www.inc.com/jeremy-quittner/dale-carnegie-centennial.html.

3. Ibid.

4. Quoted in Gil Bailie's *Violence Unveiled: Humanity at the Crossroads* (New York: Crossroad, 1995), xv, where he attributes the quotation to a conversation he had with Howard Thurman.

5. David Shaner, *The Seven Arts of Change: Leading Business Transformation That Lasts* (New York: Union Square Press, 2010), 52–53.

Chapter 6

1. "Understand the Neuroscience of Your Workforce—Improve Productivity, Products & Services," Neural Sense Neuro Marketing, July 17, 2012, http://neuralsense.word press.com/2012/07/17/understand-the-neuroscience-of-your-workforce-improve-productivity-products-services/.

2. Farhad Manjoo, "It Smelled Something Like Pizza: New Documents Reveal How Apple Really Invented the iPhone," *Slate,* September 10, 2012, www.slate.com/articles/technology/design/2012/09/iphone_design_documents_from_the_samsung_trial_reveal_more_than_ever_about_apple_s_secretive_design_process_.html.

3. The story is paraphrased from the full description offered by Sander Janssen, "Apple: Think Different," October 6, 2011, Creative Criminals, http://creativecriminals.com/print/apple-think-different/.

4. Michael J. Gelb, Kevin Carroll, and Niurka, "1-on-1: How to Inspire Creativity in Your Team," group interview, *Success,* August 10, 2009, www.success.com/articles/print/787.

5. "Understand the Neuroscience of Your Workplace."

6. David Shaner, *The Seven Arts of Change: Leading Business Transformation That Lasts* (New York: Union Square Press, 2010), 102–103.

7. Ibid., p. 101.

Chapter 7

1. "Homeless Boy Wows Judges on Korea's Got Talent," www.youtube.com/watch?v=y4CBLVNG2Q4.

2. Steve is located in Lake Oswego, Oregon. His services can be found at www.buildingchampions.com.

Chapter 8

1. Winston Churchill, "Blood, Toil, Tears and Sweat," first speech as prime minister to the House of Commons, May 13, 1940, www.winstonchurchill.org/learn/speeches/speeches-of-winston-churchill/92-blood-toil-tears-and-sweat.

2. Todd Duncan, *Time Traps: Proven Strategies for Swamped Salespeople* (Nashville, TN: Thomas Nelson, 2006), 15.

3. Al Gini, *My Job, My Self: Work and the Creation of the Modern Individual* (New York: Routledge, 2001), 2.

4. Paraphrased from the Howard Thurman quote in chapter 5.

5. While this quote is widely attributed to Wendell Berry, the original source in which he said it is unknown.

6. Proverbs 27:2a *(New International Bible,* 2011).

7. Robert Klemko, "Jake Plummer: Pat Tillman Would Hate

New NFL Rules," *USA Today,* November 11, 2012, www.usa today.com/story/sports/nfl/2012/11/11/jake-plummer-pat-tillman-would-hate-new-rules/1697131/.

8. From *Time* magazine's "Top 10 Greatest Speeches," n.d., www.time.com/time/specials/packages/article/0,28804,1841 228_1841749_1841736,00.html.

9. Steven Kotler, "Einstein at the Beach: The Hidden Relationship Between Risk and Creativity," *Forbes*, October 11, 2012, www.forbes.com/sites/stevenkotler/2012/10/11/einstein-at-the-beach-the-hidden-relationship-between-risk-and-creativity/.

10. John Lennon, from the song "Beautiful Boy (Darling Boy)," released April 11, 1981, by Geffen Records on the album *Double Fantasy.*

11. Anaïs Nin, *The Diary of Anaïs Nin,* vol. 4, *1944–1947* (Seattle, WA: Mariner Books, 1972).

Chapter 9

1. Thanks to the explanation of Asch's experiments offered by Steven Kotler, "The Secret Behind the Secret," *Psychology Today,* June 17, 2012, www.psychologytoday.com/blog/the-playing-field/201206/creativity-the-secret-behind-the-secret. A video sample of one of Asch's experiments can be found at www.youtube.com/watch?v=iRh5qy09nNw.

2. Ecclesiastes 4:12 *(New International Bible,* 2011).

3. Kotler, "The Secret Behind the Secret."

4. Gregory Berns, *Iconoclast* (Boston: Harvard Business School Press, 2010), 96.

5. Ibid., 18.

6. Mortimer Adler, *Aristotle for Everybody* (New York: Simon & Schuster, 1997).

7. Sir Ken Robinson, *The Element* (New York: Penguin Books, 2009).

8. Philip Yancey, *Soul Survivor: How Thirteen Unlikely Mentors Helped My Faith Survive the Church* (New York: Galilee/ Doubleday, 2003).

9. "Books: Orthodoxologist," review of *Gilbert Keith Chesterton,* by Maisie Ward, October 11, 1943, www.time.com/time/ magazine/article/0,9171,774701-3,00.html.

10. Margery Forester, *Michael Collins: The Lost Leader* (London: Sidgwick and Jackson, 1971), 36; P. N. Furbank, "Chesterton the Edwardian," in *G. K. Chesterton: A Centenary Appraisal,* ed. John Sullivan (New York: Harper and Row, 1974); Martin B. Green, *Gandhi: Voice of a New Age Revolution* (Mount Jackson, VA: Axios, 2009), 266.

11. Steven Pressfield, *The War of Art* (New York: Warner Books, 2003), 166.

index

about the author

Erik Wahl is an artist, author, and entrepreneur who has become a catalyst for inspiring professionals to achieve extraordinary levels of performance. He is internationally recognized as a thought-provoking graffiti artist and one of the most sought-after speakers on the corporate lecture circuit, and his process of creating "disruptive innovations" in both art and business has led to countless stories of breakthrough success. Wahl's artwork has raised millions of dollars for charities and can be seen hanging prominently in executive offices around the world. He lives with his wife and their three sons in Southern California.